Untold Stories from

WORLD WAR II
RHODE ISLAND

Untold Stories from
WORLD WAR II
RHODE ISLAND

CHRISTIAN MCBURNEY, NORMAN DESMARAIS
AND VAROUJAN KARENTZ

Bruce,   *Nov. 7, 2019*

Happy History!

[signature]

THE
History
PRESS

Published by The History Press
Charleston, SC
www.historypress.com

Front cover, clockwise from bottom left: Recruits training to use Oerlikon-Gazda antiaircraft guns on PT boats in Narragansett Bay. *Naval History and Heritage Command*; A motorboat heads out to the USS *Augusta*, the flagship of the Atlantic Fleet headquarters based in Newport, on May 2, 1941. *Naval War College Museum*; Cover page of a journal reporting crashes of aircraft taking off and landing at Naval Air Station Quonset Point from November 25, 1943, to November 4, 1944. *Providence College Library*; Aerial view of Fort Varnum, now used by the Rhode Island National Guard. It has the state's best collection of World War II fire control and other military structures. *Rhode Island Army National Guard.*
Back cover, banner: Three images from Fort Varnum. The middle photograph shows a fire-control building, and the other two show remains inside the building, including color stenciling on the wall of flags that stand for letters in the alphabet, to be used to communicate with ships offshore in the event radio communications were not possible. *Christian McBurney*; *inset*: Jim Bistodeau's flight jacket, two wartime photos of Jim and the letter Jim sent to Betty Sheldon accompanying the flight jacket, probably in early 1945. Betty carefully preserved and kept all of the items. *Marjorie Johnston*; *bottom*: Night fighter pilots at Charlestown from Squadron VF(N)-108, late summer or early fall, 1944. According to the Charlestown Historical Society, only one man in the front row survived the war. George K. Kraus, kneeling in the front row on the far right, flying out of Charlestown on a night fighter training mission on October 19, 1944, was killed in an airplane crash over Preston, Connecticut. *Charlestown Historical Society.*

First published 2019

Manufactured in the United States

ISBN 9781467141864

Library of Congress Control Number: 2019945072

Contents

Preface

By Christian McBurney and Norman Desmarais

The story of Rhode Island's extraordinary role in World War II is so big that it requires more than a single volume to tell.

As claimed in volume 1, *World War II Rhode Island*, Rhode Island's contribution to the war effort far exceeded its small size. Its greatest contribution was in training U.S. Navy officers and sailors. More than 500,000 recruits were trained at the Newport Naval Training Station; some 100,000 Seabees were trained at Davisville; more than 10,000 pilots and 1,000 Combat Information Officers received instruction at Quonset Point; and some 20,000 PT boat officers and sailors were trained at Melville. Most of these men—and some women—moved on to active theaters of war.

Rhode Island was also on the front lines. Aircraft from Quonset Point and destroyers from Newport patrolled Atlantic waters searching for German submarines. Admirals Ernest J. King and Royal E. Ingersoll, based in Newport, commanded the U.S. Navy's Atlantic Fleet (see chapter 2 in this volume).

Rhode Islanders manufactured incredible amounts of military equipment and supplies, including producing torpedoes at the Naval Torpedo Station in Newport and designing and manufacturing the first Quonset huts at West Davisville. In this volume, a chapter discussing Woonsocket's mills serves as a microcosm of the state's manufacturing contribution.

Remarkably, one sitting and four future U.S. presidents visited or trained in Rhode Island during World War II. Chapters in this volume describe President Franklin D. Roosevelt's 1940 visit to Newport, John F. Kennedy's training as a PT boat commander at Melville and George H.W. Bush's training as a pilot at Charlestown (where he wrote an affecting love letter to his new fiancée). Richard Nixon's 1942 training at Quonset Point and Harry S. Truman's 1944 campaign visit to Providence and Pawtucket are also covered.

Four chapters deal with extraordinary innovations. At Spraycliff Observatory in Jamestown, radar installed on fighter aircraft was developed, and courageous pilots stationed at Charlestown and Westerly used the radar for night fighter training. At Davisville, Seabees perfected pontoons that became a key to the D-Day landings on Normandy beaches. One pontoon they developed was a floating airfield that fighter planes tested on Narragansett Bay. At Chopmist Hill in Scituate, perhaps the nation's most successful listening spy station was established. In Woonsocket, fake rubber tanks were produced that fooled German armies. This volume also describes the Harbor Entrance Command Post at Jamestown and forts in Little Compton that helped to protect these and other facilities in the state.

There are personal stories told here too. A reporter from the *Westerly Sun* recalls how the newspaper became the first to announce the attack on Pearl Harbor. Marie Duggins narrates her uplifting experiences as a WAVE at Quonset Point. Elisabeth Sheldon befriends pilots training at Quonset Point but suffers tragedy later. Residents of the summer community of Quonochontaug fondly recall their childhood wartime memories. Edward Swain Hope breaks a racial barrier by becoming the first black man to train as a Seabee officer at Davisville. John Bradley agonizes, wondering if his spotting of German submarine *U-853* could have avoided the sinking of a merchant marine vessel off Point Judith. Quonset Point's commander, a war hero wounded commanding an aircraft carrier in the Pacific, is tragically killed in an airplane crash shortly after the war.

The final chapter identifies existing Rhode Island sites from World War II, many of which readers can visit today to deepen their appreciation of the state's exceptional contribution to the war effort.

Small state, big history, indeed!

This map shows the U.S. Navy facilities and U.S Army defenses of Narragansett Bay during World War II. Not shown are (i) thirty-one mooring buoys in the East Passage for berthing warships, (ii) the Naval Auxiliary Air Facilities at Charlestown and Westerly and (iii) concrete lookouts and fire control buildings from Little Compton to Point Judith to Watch Hill and on Block Island. *Map by Tracy Dungan.*

Acknowledgements

Each of the authors contributes to the Rhode Island history blog The Online Review of Rhode Island History at www.smallstatebighistory.com.

We wish to thank the following for helping to make this book possible: Robert Doane of the Naval War College Museum at Newport; Anne Doyle, Tom Doyle, Peter Mogielnicki and Robert Petrone of the Quonochontaug Historical Society (Quonochontaug and George H.W. Bush chapters); Pam Lyons of the Charlestown Historical Society and Cody McMillian of the George Bush Presidential Library and Museum (George H.W. Bush chapter); Irene Blais of the Woonsocket Historical Society and Rick Finkelstein (Woonsocket's mills chapter); Linsey Lee of the Martha's Vineyard Museum (Joseph Stiles and Hector Asselin interview transcripts); Nina Wright of the Westerly Public Library (*Westerly Sun*); Barbara Fallon (Robert Gentile and Benjamin York); Dianne Rugh and Rosemary Enright of the Jamestown Historical Society (Fort Burnside and Spraycliff chapters); and Professor J. David Rogers of the Missouri University of Science & Technology (pontoons chapter). Two chapters would not have been possible without the assistance of Marjorie Johnston (Elisabeth Sheldon chapter) and Linda McAuliffe (Marie Duggins chapter). Historians David Kohnen and John Hattendorf of the Naval War College Museum kindly responded to a few challenging inquiries.

We wish to thank a number of individuals for assisting in the identification of existing World War II sites in the state, in particular James A. Loffler of the Rhode Island National Guard, who gave the authors a tour of Camp Varnum, as well as the following: Christopher Zeeman, Fort Adams Museum historian and member of the Coast Defense Study Group; Pamela Gasner and Amy Dugan of the Block Island Historical Society; Vin McAloon and Keith Mitchell (Block Island tour); Thomas Klune (Fort Nathanael Greene United States Army Reserve Center); Bill Bendoaks of New England Airlines (Westerly Airport); and Cynthia Carpenter and Jack Sprengel (Quonset Point and Davisville).

The authors would like to thank librarians at the Naval History and Heritage Command Library in Washington, D.C., Providence College Library (with its Quonset Point collection), Museum of Work and Culture in Woonsocket, Rhode Island Historical Society and U.S. Navy Seabee Museum.

The authors thank a coauthor of the first volume of *World War II Rhode Island*, R. John Kennedy, and the smallstatebighistory.com website's copyeditor, Mary Keane, for reviewing draft chapters of this book. Any remaining mistakes are those of the authors.

President Franklin D. Roosevelt Inspects Newport, August 1940

By Christian McBurney

Rhode Islanders were thrilled when on August 12, 1940, Franklin D. Roosevelt arrived in Narragansett Bay onboard the presidential yacht USS *Potomac*. The president steamed to the state to inspect the navy's expanding military facilities, particularly in Newport. At this time, Roosevelt's official position was to try to keep the United States out of the war in Europe. He felt this stance was necessary for him to win election for an unprecedented third term as president. He had just been nominated by the Democratic Party and was about to embark on a difficult campaign against the Republican nominee, Wendell Willkie. Roosevelt also wanted to see for himself the navy's war readiness in case an incident drew the United States into the war against Germany—or with Japan. Many agreed with FDR that a strong defense was the best way to avoid being attacked. Finally, the president wanted to remind the state's voters of the increased military spending allocated to the state. Meanwhile, the Battle of Britain had commenced, with hundreds of British and German warplanes battling in the skies over England.

On the final leg of a three-day inspection of New England military bases, the president's yacht arrived from Boston in Narragansett Bay at 1:00 a.m. on Monday and anchored off Jamestown. The small party accompanying the president on his yacht included his close aide Secretary of Commerce Harry Hopkins, Secretary of the Navy Frank Knox, naval aide Captain Daniel Callaghan and U.S. Senator David Walsh from Massachusetts.

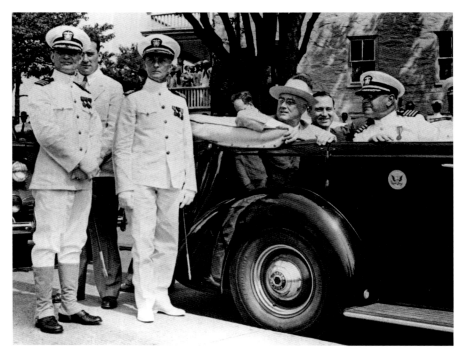

President Roosevelt about to be driven to review navy recruits on the grounds of the Naval Training Station at Newport on August 12, 1940, with Secretary of the Navy Frank Knox, Senator Theodore F. Green and Admiral Edward C. Kalbfus. *FDR Library.*

Morning fog delayed the president's tour. President Roosevelt later said that his party spent some time fishing. He added that Knox and Walsh caught some mackerel, but he came up empty.

Finally, at 9:05 a.m., *Potomac* pulled up to the East Dock on Goat Island, the 23-acre, closely guarded home of the Naval Torpedo Station. Most of the U.S. Navy's torpedoes were produced at this site. Upon disembarking, Roosevelt posed for a photograph with Captain Callaghan. Callaghan had two years and three months to live—as a rear admiral, he went down with his heavy cruiser in action at Guadalcanal.

Ready to greet the president was a coterie of prominent Rhode Island politicians: U.S. Senator Theodore Francis Green, Governor William H. Vanderbilt and Newport mayor Henry Wheeler. These men huddled with Roosevelt and officers of the Torpedo Station and Naval War College below decks until 9:32 a.m. When the meeting ended, Roosevelt started his inspection, joined by a few more local officials, including U.S. District

Attorney and rising Democratic politician (and the next state governor) J. Howard McGrath.

Riding in an open car with Governor Vanderbilt and Senator Green, and in a jovial mood, Roosevelt first visited the officers' quarters at the southern end of Goat Island, cheered on by the officers' wives and children. Some 194 marines dressed in khaki and armed with rifles and bayonets lined the president's route to the torpedo factory, as did about 100 officers from the Training Station in summer white uniforms. Secret Service agents in a separate car followed the president. Roosevelt chatted animatedly with Captain Thomas Withers, the factory commandant, throughout his tour.

The 4,100 military and civilian employees at the torpedo factory, on shifts keeping the facility producing twenty-four hours a day, were under orders to continue working during the president's visit. Peering through the factory windows, Roosevelt saw an assembly production line. He showed a keen interest in two of the latest torpedoes shown to him. He was informed that each weighed a ton and a half and cost $10,000. They were painted yellow, indicating they were unarmed duds.

The president chatted briefly with Captain Withers on how to increase production. Roosevelt then said, "All right Tom, let's go." The chief executive's visit on Goat Island lasted only about thirty minutes. Meanwhile, workmen who left their posts and had gathered at the windows broke out in spontaneous applause, while thousands cheered him from Long Wharf.

A small navy barge carried Roosevelt and his party from Goat Island to Coasters Harbor Island. On the way, Roosevelt admired at their moorings five destroyers engaged in neutrality patrols, monitoring German U-boat activity off the United States' East Coast. A massive twin-motored PBY seaplane, also used in neutrality patrols, took off from the harbor's waters, sprayed water in elegant arcs and roared west over Conanicut Island. In July, Roosevelt had ordered that the destroyers and seaplanes begin to convoy American shipping to Britain.

Roosevelt landed on Coasters Harbor Island near a barracks under construction at about 10:20 a.m. On the green hills of Dewey Field, 1,500 Training Station recruits and officers dressed in white uniforms stood at attention in neat rows as the sun broke through the fog. Following the national anthem and a twenty-one-gun salute, the sailors marched off the field singing "Roll Out the Barrel," while the president and his party chuckled.

The president, dressed in a gray suit and sporting a Panama hat, and the other dignitaries piled into two open cars to inspect the Naval Training Station and Naval War College buildings. They drove as far as Coddington

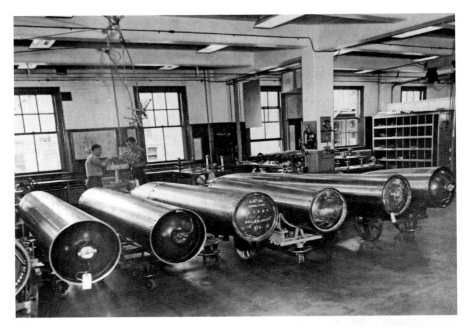

A room filled with torpedoes in production at the Newport Torpedo Station on Goat Island. President Roosevelt may have seen such a scene when he looked through the windows of a station building. *Naval War College Museum.*

Point. Riding with the president and answering his questions were Admiral Edward Kalbfus, president of the Naval War College, and Captain Leo Welch, commanding officer of the Training Station. After his quick tour, Roosevelt shook hands with officers and their families, adding a personal word to several of them.

The president was then driven to a wharf where stood the three-masted frigate USS *Constellation*, said to have fought in the War of 1812 and still used in training. Its commander, retired Lieutenant John Davis of Newport, recipient of the Congressional Medal of Honor for cutting the cable of an enemy warship in the Spanish-American War, presented a piece of oak beam from the ship. The pleased president said he would add it to his naval souvenirs collection at his Hyde Park museum. Davis informed his distinguished visitor that his fondest wish was to have the old vessel recommissioned. Knowing that the three-masted USS *Constitution* anchored at Boston was a commissioned navy vessel, Roosevelt declared, "Why not?" Eight days later, he signed the order. During the war at Newport, *Constellation* temporarily served as the flagship for the Atlantic Fleet.

Navy recruits marching on Dewey Field, Newport Naval Training Station, with USS *Constellation* in the background, circa 1941. *Naval History and Heritage Command, Photography Division.*

Completing his short tour by about 11:10 a.m., the chief executive held a press conference for the assembled journalists in front of *Constellation*. "This carries me back to 1917," the president reminisced after his tour. Here FDR referred to a visit to Newport he made on September 5, 1917, as assistant navy secretary during World War I.

Declaring himself satisfied with the readiness of the Torpedo Station and Training Station, Roosevelt promised that Newport would soon again become a "main center" of naval activity, as it had been in World War I. The president announced that when another 1,000 workers were hired to work at the Torpedo Station, torpedo production would be "well up to schedule." He also said that when the barracks and mess hall under construction were completed, another 1,000 sailors could be trained at the Training Station at one time. Captain Welch added that there were then about 2,100 trainees. It was also announced that the president had approved a grant of $1,100,000 for the construction of 252 dwelling units in Newport to help meet the housing shortage due to the Training Station's expansion.

Joking with the press, Roosevelt chided Senator Green, known for promoting military spending in the state, for "asking too much for Rhode Island." He then said that Governor Vanderbilt "used to be one of the kids around here." Turning to Vanderbilt, a member of one of the wealthiest and most socially prominent families in the nation, he joked, "You were a seaman second class, weren't you, Bill?" The Republican governor smiled but made no response. In fact, Vanderbilt had served as a midshipman in the navy during the war—enlisting in 1917 at the age of just fifteen.

Only officers' families, civilian workers and the personnel of the Torpedo Station, Training Station and the Naval War College got a close look at the president. In addition to the large crowd gathered on Long Wharf, other groups of spectators gathered at Biggs Wharf, smaller wharves jutting into the bay, Battery Park, Washington Street and the causeway leading to the Training Station.

The president took the admiral's barge back to Goat Island. At 11:40 a.m., Roosevelt boarded *Potomac*, and ten minutes later, the vessel was headed south in Narragansett Bay. Rounding Beavertail Point at the southern tip of Conanicut Island, the president's yacht turned to the north and passed under the newly built Jamestown Bridge, formally dedicated just a few weeks earlier. Roosevelt wanted to view construction at the Quonset Point Naval Air Station farther north. At his news conference, he said he would look at Quonset "as closely as possible without going ashore because it's one of our most important developments just now."

Potomac had a diverse escort. A tanker from the Newport Oil Corporation was in "full holiday dress for the occasion," according to the *Newport Mercury*. The newspaper report continued, "A small fishing boat, with a large American flag, hovered nearby, and a number of power craft followed the naval launches up and down the bay. Whistles tooted as the President went up the harbor." Two coast guard cutters escorted *Potomac*, making sure the private boats did not get too close. The few summer residents still allowed at Quonset Point unfurled a huge American flag. Several hundred onlookers lined the waterfront, but Roosevelt did not disembark. The president commented that the navy had selected a good site for an air station. Within a year, Quonset Point would become the largest naval air station in the Northeast.

As Roosevelt then made his way out of Narragansett Bay, headed to New London to review submarine facilities, he was joined by four submarines and a destroyer. The navy blimp *K-2*, from the Naval Air Station at Lakehurst, New Jersey, flew over *Potomac*, following it up and down the bay.

Roosevelt never visited Newport again. If he had, he would have been amazed at the tremendous expansion of the wartime naval facilities. By 1945, more than eleven thousand workers produced torpedoes at the Torpedo Station, and Training Station facilities were increased, permitting more than six thousand sailors to be trained at Newport at one time.

2

Admirals King and Ingersoll Command the Atlantic Fleet from Newport

By Christian McBurney

Of the top Allied leaders of World War II, Fleet Admiral Ernest J. King was perhaps the most difficult with whom to work. He always seemed annoyed, partly because of his unwavering advocacy on behalf of the U.S. Navy in his dealings with the U.S. Army and with Great Britain. King agreed that the defeat of Germany was the number one priority in the war, but he fought hard to divert substantial resources from Europe to the Pacific theater of war, believing (correctly) that Japan could be defeated at the same time. He succeeded in building a powerful U.S. Navy and logistics structure that helped destroy the German U-boat menace in the Atlantic and defeated the Imperial Japanese Navy.

Born in Lorain, Ohio, in 1878, King graduated from the U.S. Naval Academy in 1901 and later served as an officer in World War I. He was assigned to the Naval War College at Newport twice, once as a student and later as an instructor.

King rose through the ranks, obtaining experience with naval aviation and submarines, as well as with surface ships. (The first time he flew in an airplane was from the rear cockpit of an open-air bi-winged seaplane taking off and landing on Narragansett Bay in 1926.) On February 1, 1941, King was appointed commander in chief, Atlantic Fleet, with the rank of full admiral. Now sixty-two years old, he had to select his headquarters. Wanting to be both near to Washington, D.C., to get there on short notice, and close to sea operations, he chose Newport, Rhode Island.

Next, King had to choose his flagship. The heavy cruiser USS *Augusta*, carrying 8-inch guns, arrived in Narragansett Bay in late April. On this book's cover is a photograph of a watercolor painting by marine artist Ian Marshall showing *Augusta* on May 2, 1941, the day that Admiral King broke his four-star flag in *Augusta* as commander in chief of the U.S. Atlantic Fleet. The ship is moored to a large buoy with Conanicut Island (Jamestown) visible to the left (west), King's preferred location. The Naval War College is in the distant background (to the right, east). Two ship's boats are approaching—perhaps from Government Landing in Newport or from other ships—to join three already riding to a boom.

A single telephone line to *Augusta* served as the admiral's only communication with the mainland. Sometimes it broke in the current. King once summoned a station officer and instructed him, "You will keep that line in service if you have to keep a boatload of repairmen at the buoy twenty-four hours a day." King also had the warship fitted out with an early radar system, showing what it could do.

Admiral Ernest J. King onboard USS *Augusta*, his flagship while he served in Newport. Next to King is Secretary of the Navy Frank Knox. *Naval History and Heritage Command*.

In late May, King received the electrifying news that the German battleship *Bismarck* was on the prowl in the Atlantic for British vessels to sink. He ordered long-range naval seaplanes to Argentia, Newfoundland, in Canada to join in the search for the ship. To minimize publicity and avoid criticism that the United States was getting involved in the war, King issued orders for the seaplanes not to land on Narragansett Bay. Nevertheless, the pilot of one of them did find it necessary to do just that. As his seaplane taxied past *Augusta*, the pilot joked, "Admiral, there must be a Narragansett Bay in Newfoundland." "There had better be," King quipped loudly.

In August 1941, King handled the secret arrangements to transport President Roosevelt and his entourage to Newfoundland for the president's first wartime summit with Winston Churchill. King had *Augusta* fitted out with ramps for the president's wheelchair. On August 5, Roosevelt boarded *Augusta* from the presidential yacht *Potomac* at sea. The *Augusta* proceeded north to Placentia Bay with a small escort of navy warships. On Augusta 9, Churchill was ferried to *Augusta*. After the two leaders shook hands, a moment of silence passed until Churchill said, "At long last, Mr. President," to which Roosevelt replied, "Glad to have you aboard, Mr. Churchill." On August 10, they signed the Atlantic Charter, summarizing their war aims.

On occasion, King found it necessary take the overnight train from Kingston Station to the nation's capital for two weeks. "Well," he would tell his staff officers at Newport, "I've got to go down to Washington again to straighten out those dumb bastards once more."

From Newport, King directed the undeclared warfare against German U-boats that threatened American shipping to Great Britain. His forces included destroyers based in Newport and seaplanes operating out of newly constructed hangars at Quonset Point. Throughout 1941, they escorted U.S. supply ships on voyages to Britain and patrolled the country's neutrality zone, which extended three hundred miles off the East Coast. "We are no longer in peace time status," King proclaimed to his officers at sea.

U-boat commanders were under orders not to fire on U.S. vessels for fear of provoking an incident that could propel the United States to enter the war against Germany. Following Hitler's invasion of the Soviet Union in June, Roosevelt ordered the navy to expand its convoys to two hundred miles west of Iceland. Beginning on September 1, Roosevelt extended the line to Iceland itself, increasing the risk of conflicts with U-boats. Three days later, a U-boat fired two torpedoes at the destroyer USS *Greer*, which counterattacked with depth charges. Neither vessel was damaged, but it was the first exchange of live ammunition between United States and

German naval forces. On October 17, in a night attack against a convoy, another U-boat sent a torpedo into the destroyer *Kearny*, killing 11 sailors and wounding 22. The engagement marked the first shedding of American blood in combat in World War II. On October 31, off the coast of Iceland, a U-boat fired a single torpedo at the destroyer *Reuben James*, breaking it in two and sending it to the bottom, with the loss of 115 men (including all the officers) out of a crew of 160. The *Kearny* was the first U.S. Navy vessel lost to enemy action in World War II. Although a naval aide later wrote that the deaths "shook him up," an undeterred King ordered the convoys to continue, driving his Atlantic Fleet hard. In November, King's stern image appeared in *Life* magazine under the caption "King of the Atlantic."

On December 7, 1941, *Augusta* was moored at buoy 7, next to the Naval War College, when in the afternoon the shocking news of the Japanese bombing of Pearl Harbor was brought to King. King was not, however, on his flagship. He was at the Reading Room, a private men's club that still thrives in Newport. Perhaps he was sipping whiskey. He rushed over to Luce Hall to meet with his old friend Admiral Edward Kalbfus, then serving both as the president of the Naval War College and commander of Naval Operating Base Newport. The two received what King called "the latest dope" from Washington, D.C., about the attack.

King ordered a staff officer to be ready for them to travel to Washington, D.C., the next day. Traveling in his civilian clothes as usual, King took the express train from Kingston Station. He ignored the report that enemy bombers were bound for New York City, accurately assessing it was a false alarm. On December 10, he met with President Roosevelt, Secretary of the Navy Frank Knox and others. After returning to Newport, on December 14 he again took a train from Kingston back to the nation's capital, meeting with Roosevelt that evening. The next day, Roosevelt offered King the post of commander in chief of the U.S. Fleet, and King accepted.

After Roosevelt signed the order appointing King on December 18, Secretary Knox called King the right man to transform the U.S. Navy from its defensive posture into an offensive one. King had his own take about the shakeup in leadership, explaining that "when the going gets tough, they call in the sons-of-bitches!" Meanwhile, after meeting with Roosevelt on December 16 and 18, King returned to Newport and packed his bags. On December 20, he took a navy plane from Quonset Point to Washington, D.C., where he would be based the rest of the war. On Christmas Day, a gunboat, the USS *Vixen*, departed Newport with the rest of King's belongings and papers on board, headed for Washington Navy Yard. Three months after departing

Newport, Roosevelt appointed King as chief of naval operations. King served in both positions for the remainder of the war. Congress promoted him to fleet admiral in December 1944.

Handpicked by King, Vice Admiral Royal E. Ingersoll replaced him as commander in chief, U.S. Atlantic Fleet, on January 1, 1942. Ingersoll came from Indiana and a long line of navy officers. His son, a lieutenant, would be killed at the Battle of Midway.

As King had, Ingersoll used Newport as his headquarters. He was assisted by his chief of staff, Rear Admiral Olaf M. Hustvedt, twelve staff members and sixteen junior-grade officers, all working day and night. Ingersoll's aides estimated they sent more than 150 dispatches and 100 letters a day.

Ingersoll organized the movements of thousands of ships carrying men and supplies across the Atlantic at the precise hour for the landings on the North African coast in November 1942. No troop ships were lost, despite the best attempts of German U-boats. Ingersoll next oversaw the Atlantic Fleet running troop convoys and transporting stores, munitions and fuel in the massive buildup in Great Britain for D-Day and the campaigns in Sicily and Italy. He also helped to maintain a blockade on Germany and watched for German surface ships prowling the Atlantic.

Ingersoll directed the Atlantic Fleet's antisubmarine war, which was a matter of primary concern since the outbreak of hostilities. The Battle of the Atlantic was too vast and complex to be directed by Ingersoll and his small staff in Newport. He was aided in his efforts by the Eastern Seaboard Frontier headquarters in New York City and, starting in early 1943, a group located at King's headquarters in Washington, D.C. "Admiral Ingersoll is generally credited with whipping the U-boat menace and with solving the vast Atlantic logistics problem," his Navy Department biography states.

Ingersoll planned to use a three-thousand-ton converted gunboat, *Vixen*, as his auxiliary flagship once it returned from Washington, D.C., after repairs. In the meantime, he transferred his staff and three-star flag to USS *Constellation*, a three-masted sailing ship moored next to the Naval War College (thought to have fought in the War of 1812, it was later determined to have been constructed in 1855). His quarters, in the captain's cabin in the stern of the frigate, were furnished with antiques and green carpeting. In July 1942, he was commissioned a full admiral and broke his flag at the mizzen of *Constellation*. After departing *Constellation*, Ingersoll told a news reporter, "Personally, I have never had a more enjoyable time on any ship." But Ingersoll was glad to see *Vixen* enter Newport Harbor in July 1942. He was anxious to steam along the East Coast to visit navy facilities, rather than

Vice Admiral Royal Ingersoll (*left*) replaced King as commander of the Atlantic Fleet and was also based in Newport. He is walking with his chief of staff, Rear Admiral Olaf M. Hustvedt, in 1942 in Newport onboard USS *Constellation*, which often served as Ingersoll's flagship. Hustvedt also served as King's chief of staff. *Naval History and Heritage Command.*

have his officers "come to the 'mountain,'" as he put it. Ingersoll's formal flagship became the cruiser USS *Augusta*, but he preferred to have it engaged outside of Newport in active operations.

The taciturn Ingersoll ably served in Newport until November 1944. With the battle against German U-boats effectively won, King appointed him logistics czar of the West Coast. (Ingersoll's replacement did not use Newport as his headquarters.) Ingersoll advanced to the rank of admiral the following July. He was later awarded the Distinguished Service Medal and cited as a "forceful and resolute leader." Ingersoll should be celebrated as one of the top U.S. Navy admirals of World War II.

3

Chopmist Hill Listening Post

RHODE ISLAND'S SPY STATION

By Norman Desmarais

Three months after Rhode Islanders swarmed into the streets with other joyous Americans celebrating the end of World War II, the *Providence Journal* publicized the state's top-secret role in defeating Germany and Japan. It was a tale of espionage, now virtually forgotten, centered on, of all places, a farmhouse in Scituate.

In 1940, Great Britain was at war with Germany virtually alone, but many thought it inevitable that the United States would join the conflict. The country was already fortifying the British with supplies and weaponry. A year before the attack on Pearl Harbor, the Radio Intelligence Division of the Federal Communications Commission (FCC) charged Thomas B. Cave, a Boston radio technician, with finding a hilltop in southern New England that could serve as one of several listening posts to detect shortwave radio transmissions from German spies in the United States. Cave found one in Greenville, Rhode Island, but looking further, as he drove up Darby Road in Scituate, he found a more suitable site. The area was devoid of all interference from power lines or other factors that could interfere with radio transmissions. He thought that 730-foot Chopmist Hill, the state's second-highest point, was an ideal site to monitor enemy radio transmissions. From these humble beginnings, Chopmist Hill Listening Post ended up becoming perhaps the most important listening post in the nation's mainland forty-eight states.

The FCC leased William A. Suddard's fourteen-room farmhouse and 183 acres of land on Chopmist Hill in March 1941 for the duration of the war. Workers began erecting scores of telephone poles across the property, sinking them nine feet deep to keep them below the tree line, making them almost impossible to detect from the air or from any considerable distance on the ground. They strung some 85,000 feet of antenna wire—the equivalent of sixteen miles—around the poles and wired it into the house. Civilian linemen from the Narragansett Electric Company frequently changed the configuration of the antenna pole mounts, sometimes only a few feet, to improve reception, unaware of their true function.

Foreman Charlie Weinert must have been frustrated by Cave's constant requests to change the antenna pole mounts. After the war, when the station was declassified, Cave told Weinert, "Every time you moved those poles you were following Rommel as he was backing up across North Africa." Weinert replied, "If I had known that, I'd have dug poles all the way to Cairo."

Chopmist's rooms were filled with banks of sensitive radio receivers, transmitters and related equipment. The grounds outside the main building also included two long-range direction-finding antennae that could be rotated to get a bearing on the transmitting station. This information, when compared with similar measurements from other receivers located at distant stations, allowed the transmitting location to be triangulated. Called an Adcock DF, each wooden structure had stairs leading up to a platform with a shack on top of it containing the direction finder equipment. The antenna was affixed to the top of the shack's roof.

Thomas Cave claimed that from Chopmist Hill he could pinpoint the location of any radio transmission in the country within fifteen minutes. Skeptical military officials conducted some 127 tests for him to prove his claims. In one of them, the army hung a wire out a window at the Pentagon to transmit a signal without telling the FCC. The object was to see how long it would take various receiving stations to detect this signal. Cave, detecting the signal's origin within only seven minutes, reported that the Pentagon had a spy within its midst.

Because of some geographic and atmospheric anomalies, the station could intercept radio transmissions coming from Europe, South America and Africa with a clarity of reception shared by no other station in the country. Chopmist Hill was the largest and most successful of the thirteen similar facilities around the country. They included Fort Ward in Washington, D.C.; Winter Harbor, Maine; Amagansett, New York; Cheltenham, Maryland; and Jupiter, Florida.

Chopmist was a top-secret facility. Workers fenced off the perimeter and erected floodlights. Armed guards patrolled the property's perimeter and

The former top-secret Chopmist Listening Post is now a private residence. *Norman Desmarais.*

kept a careful watch to safeguard the station's wartime operation. Anyone visiting the farmhouse—and only guests who had official business were permitted—had to arrive with a state police escort.

There is very little official information available about the listening post. Information on Chopmist, still classified, will not be released until 2049.

The station's primary function was listening to enemy radio messages worldwide twenty-four hours a day. Operators monitored more than four hundred different enemy radio transmitting stations broadcasting on any given day. They ferreted out secret low-frequency transmissions hidden under the beams of commercial radio stations abroad. Enciphered messages were forwarded electronically to Washington, D.C., for deciphering.

Chopmist Hill and other monitoring stations pinpointed the location of virtually every German radio transmitter and intercepted most wartime messages sent by German spies working in the United States. Spies could use compact short-wave transmitters that were strong enough to be heard across the Atlantic Ocean. Often spies were allowed to continue operating so that counterintelligence officers could run down their sources of information. This work was perhaps a major reason why the United States suffered almost no sabotage by enemy agents.

Many German spies sought safe haven in South American countries. But they were still monitored by Chopmist and other stations in the United States. In one instance, a message intercepted at Chopmist and conveyed to the British resulted in a British request to monitor a frequency on which it was anticipated that arrangements would be made to land an agent in South America from a German submarine. In another case, on October 21, 1941, Chopmist intercepted a radio transmission from South Africa to Portugal. Thomas Cave passed on the information, which led to the discovery of a Nazi spy in West Africa. The Scituate post also uncovered a German spy transmitting from a Portuguese colony in West Africa to his German handler in Lisbon, Portugal.

One of the station's most important jobs was to intercept German weather reports, which proved vital for bombing raids over Germany. The reports, broadcast at a frequency undetectable in Great Britain, were easily picked up across the Atlantic at Chopmist Hill.

Chopmist Hill picked up German transmissions to Field Marshal Erwin Rommel's tanks in the North African desert and relayed German battlefield strategy intercepts to the British, who, under Field Marshal Bernard Montgomery, ultimately defeated Rommel at El Alamein.

The station also guided home stray planes and helped in air-sea rescue operations almost nightly. When a transport plane carrying twenty-two wounded men back from Europe was forced down in northern Labrador, in remote Canada, it was able to make contact with the air transport command (ATC) station in Presque Isle, Maine. The ATC immediately put the Scituate monitors to work establishing the exact position of the lost aircraft. Rescue planes ran into difficulties—they flew so close to the magnetic North Pole that their compasses were rendered useless. The twelve to fifteen planes sent on the search mission relied on the Scituate station to keep from getting lost themselves. Finally, the downed plane was discovered, but it took three weeks before a rescue ship actually reached the spot and three months for the last man to be rescued.

Chopmist also located seamen adrift on lifeboats equipped with radio. When shipwreck victims had no radio but were located by rescue planes,

Chopmist operators took bearings on the plane, which circled the victims. Nearby ships were dispatched to the spot.

Chopmist Hill station, in collaboration with a clandestine station outside Rio de Janeiro in Brazil, is also credited with saving *Queen Mary*, the pride of Britain's maritime fleet. While the ship was docked in Rio de Janeiro for fuel and supplies in March 1942, local German spies learned its future course and alerted their superiors. As *Queen Mary* was about to sail to Australia with ten thousand Allied troops onboard, the Chopmist station intercepted orders from Germany to a German submarine wolf pack operating in the south Atlantic to sink the ship. Chopmist Hill operators alerted the British, enabling the British Admiralty to change *Queen Mary*'s route.

Chopmist picked up signals from Japanese balloons in the Pacific Ocean. Japan released some nine thousand balloons loaded with dynamite designed to follow the jet stream to the United States and detonate in sensitive areas. The balloons had electronic tracking devices permitting the Japanese to monitor their positions, which meant that Chopmist operators could too. With this information, Allied fighter pilots shot down many balloons. The only casualties from the Japanese balloon operation occurred in Oregon, when a woman and five children on a Sunday school picnic were killed after they tried to take a bomb apart.

The ability to copy signals sent by Nazi spies using low-power transmissions through interference was an invaluable skill. After the war, the chief of the Radio Intelligence Division, George E. Sterling, wrote, "at times while inspecting stations, I listened in on some of the clandestine networks and saw monitoring officers, like Tom Cave at Scituate, R.I., make solid copy of code groups when I could hardly hear or follow the signals that were being copied."

Sometimes the monitors' work was extremely challenging. Thomas Cave wrote the following about Chopmist operators copying transmissions between Madrid, Spain, and Berlin, Germany, starting in the summer of 1944:

Copying Madrid was quite a strain for even our oldest and most experienced men. It was nerve wracking to copy a signal like that, as weak as it was, under all kinds of interference, constantly changing frequency, and sometimes with heavy lightning crashes and local tropical rain static to worsen matters. The newer men here were not very successful as interference caused them to miss 50 to 100 words at a time. One of our younger men threw the headset on the floor, got his lunch kit and went home, saying "if I have to copy that any longer I will shoot myself." A couple of days off and the non-assignment to that type of work put him "back to normal." As the case continued, and the traffic got heavier from Madrid to Berlin toward the end of the war, some of us began to get "dit crazy" and it was necessary to put only the steadiest men on the case. And then only to allow them to cover it a half week, that is, 24 hours per week.

Chopmist Hill's remarkable radio capabilities captured world attention in January 1946 when seven inspectors from the newly formed United Nations Organization were appointed to recommend a site for its headquarters and an airport. As they examined Chopmist, Thomas Cave told them it was "the best location in the country for radio transmission and reception to any part of the world." In 1946, when John D. Rockefeller, Jr. offered United Nations officials $8.5 million to purchase a six-block tract of land along the East River, they settled on New York City.

In 1951, the FCC moved the Chopmist Hill station to Millis, Massachusetts. The State of Rhode Island took over the property, using it as the state's civil defense headquarters for about fifteen years. Eventually, the property reverted to private ownership.

John F. Kennedy Trains at Melville, October 1942 to January 1943

By Christian McBurney

On March 11, 1942, Lieutenant John D. Bulkeley broke through Japanese navy lines with his squadron of PT boats to pick up and transport General Douglas MacArthur and his family, as well as his staff, from Corregidor and Bataan in the Philippine Islands to Mindanao Island. From there, MacArthur was flown to Australia to assume overall command of the U.S. Army in the Pacific. Bulkeley's brave feat was one of the few bright spots for the U.S. military early in the war. Brought back to the United States, Bulkeley was showered with a ticker tape parade down Seventh Avenue in New York on May 13, and President Roosevelt awarded him the Medal of Honor.

Between May and September 1942, Bulkeley served as a training officer at the Motor Torpedo Boat Squadrons Training Center at Melville in Portsmouth, Rhode Island, the nation's only PT boat training facility. He spent most of his time on barnstorming tours speaking to the public, trying to sell war bonds and recruiting young men for the PT boat service. On July 22, Bulkeley crossed Narragansett Bay and gave a speech to an appreciative crowd of officers at Naval Air Station Quonset Point.

John Harllee, a senior instructor at Melville who had been a PT boat skipper at Pearl Harbor when it was bombed, sometimes accompanied Bulkeley to colleges. He recalled how effective Bulkeley was talking to students: "He told them, 'Only one in ten of you will return from the war if you are selected to be a PT-boat skipper.' Then the entire group would rush forward to volunteer."

Twenty-five-year-old John F. Kennedy, when attending Naval Reserve Officers Training School at Northwestern University in Chicago, listened raptly to an inspiring presentation by Bulkeley in September 1942. Kennedy then desperately wanted to become a PT boat commander. JFK had an ace up his sleeve: his wealthy and influential father, Joseph P. Kennedy. The former ambassador to Great Britain arranged a lunch meeting with Bulkeley to persuade the famed PT boat commander to take his son. Bulkeley agreed to interview Kennedy. A pleased Joseph Kennedy added that, as Bulkeley recalled, "He hoped Jack could be sent someplace that wasn't too deadly." With JFK's Harvard University degree, sailing experience, stellar marks earned at Naval Reserve Officers Training School and his eagerness to "get in combat with the enemy as soon as possible," Bulkeley was impressed and did not need to be pressured.

On October 1, 1942, Kennedy began his training at the Motor Torpedo Boat Squadrons Training Center at Melville. On October 10, he was promoted to the rank of lieutenant, junior grade. One classmate recalled Kennedy sometimes inviting fellow officers sharing his Quonset hut to nearby Hyannis, on Cape Cod, to join him for a touch football game and walks on the beach. Another bunkmate recalled Kennedy teaching him to place newspapers under his cot's mattress to help stave off cold temperatures.

Kennedy never described his Melville experiences, but two officers of PT boats who crossed paths with Kennedy near Guadalcanal did. William F. "Bud" Liebenow captained the PT boat that rescued Kennedy and his stranded crew of *PT-109*, and Donald B. Frost commanded a PT boat that sometimes went on patrol with Kennedy's *PT-109*. They recalled their days at Melville in 2005. Liebenow told an interviewer:

> [John D.] *Bulkeley came to Northwestern and recruited people for PTs. We had a lot of volunteers. And I got accepted and, of course, went to Melville, which is the PT Boat Training Center. And we went through boat handling and all kinds of exercises and training for the boats to learn how to operate them....*
>
> *I think* [most] *all the PT officers went through Melville....And at Melville we got up at five o'clock in the morning, we had P.E., physical exercise, ate breakfast, and then started classes. Between each class we got, I think, a five-minute break.*

The class of December 1942 at the Motor Torpedo Squadrons Training Center at Melville, in Portsmouth. John F. Kennedy is in the back row, seventh from the right, October 1942. *John F. Kennedy Presidential Library and Museum.*

We lived in Quonset huts. And I can't recall how many were in a Quonset hut, but it was probably, I think, maybe 20 guys. We had two lines of bunks down each side, and they were three feet apart; actually they were cots. And we trained in Narragansett Bay, took the boats out. PT boats only operate at night. And so most of our training was done at night. Of course, we started out in the daytime because a lot of us didn't know what a boat was. [Laughter] *Some of us, a lot of people in PTs were experienced sailors and Ivy League college graduates, which Jack* [Kennedy] *was....*

And the training at Melville was very good. It saved us, I guess, so we knew what we were doing. It was rigorous training.

Frost recalled:

[W]*ithin a couple of weeks we were sent down to Melville, Rhode Island, which is just this side of Newport. This again was in the middle of the winter, which is a rough place, going back to Newport in the wintertime* [Frost had attended the Naval Training Station at Newport the winter before]....[W]*e had a lot of snow as well as the cold. But we graduated from PT boats. I think it was like 12 weeks we were in Melville.*

There was a nice training center there. It had nice docks. And we had boats that we could ride on and get the experience. And we went through all of the different classes. There was a lot more to it than just training or the engine work. Because if you were in a small crew of say 12 people on a PT boat, you couldn't just say, well, I only work on engines, nothing else. You had to learn how to work on guns because you were going to be firing the guns, and you had to be able to clean guns and so forth. You also had to know something about navigation and something about torpedoes and the whole bit. So we went through a lot of various classes in operating the PT boats. Then after graduation from that, they sent us to our squadrons.

Frost continued:

[T]he officers [like Kennedy] *had to know all the same things, too. Because they were in charge of the whole works. So if anything went wrong, they had to have some idea as to what needed to be done. So they had all gone through some sort of officer training anyway. Most of them were college fellows, not long out of college either.*

Frost discussed some weapons used on PT boats that had Rhode Island connections: torpedoes produced at the Naval Torpedo Station on Goat Island and Oerlikon-Gazda antiaircraft guns manufactured in Rhode Island:

[W]e had four torpedo tubes, and these were the big, old torpedoes. These were leftovers from World War I. At that time they decided that they would put them into mothballs on Torpedo Island [Goat Island], *which is located in Narragansett Bay, not too far from where Melville is. And they would take these torpedoes, and every so many months or years or whatever, they would go through them and upgrade them and change the mechanism or whatever needed to be done. And those were the torpedoes that we started off with on PT boats. Sorry to say, a lot of them didn't work too well, and they didn't do what they were supposed to do, and they didn't function. There were a lot of problems with those until finally* [torpedo tubes] *were removed* [from PT boats] *later in the war....*

The stern now, where we did have what we called a 20mm gun that was called an Oerlikon gun. It was a German-style gun, I guess. That was on a higher pedestal and could swing around, and you could fire...both sides and the stern.

Kennedy performed so well in his classes that upon completing his training on December 2, Lieutenant Harllee ordered him to remain as a training instructor rather than ship out to the front lines overseas. Kennedy was assigned his first command, *PT-101*, a seventy-eight-foot Higgins boat that was part of Motor Torpedo Boat Squadron Four, then operating out of Melville. Kennedy sped up and down Narragansett Bay on patrol and in training sessions many times.

In January 1943, *PT-101* and four other PT boats were dispatched to Panama, Florida. Seeking combat duty, Kennedy used his own contacts to be transferred on February 23 as a replacement officer to Motor Torpedo Boat Squadron Two, based at Tulagi Island off Guadalcanal. There Kennedy showed excellent leadership skills in commanding his crew, although the PT boats were overmatched when confronting Japanese destroyers.

Before leaving on his fateful cruise aboard *PT-109*, Kennedy filled out his crew with recent arrivals from Melville. *PT-109*, commanded by Kennedy, was one of fifteen boats sent out on patrol on the night of August 1–2, 1943, to intercept Japanese warships seeking to supply Japanese troops on nearby islands. At around 2:00 a.m., with Kennedy at the helm, in poor visibility and with his boat's engines roaring, the Japanese destroyer *Amagiri* traveling at forty knots cut *PT-109* in two. The impact threw Kennedy into the cockpit, where he landed on his bad back. Still, Kennedy helped some of his sailors who had been badly burned swim to safety to a small island three miles away. The collision killed two crewmen, but the remaining eleven survivors made it to the island.

After swimming to larger Nauru Island, Kennedy and his executive officer found natives serving as coast watchers supporting the Americans. Kennedy wrote a message on a coconut for one of the native scouts, Biuku Gasa, to take to the nearest navy base. The coconut said: "11 alive native knows posit & reef Nauru Island Kennedy." Bud Liebenow's *PT-157* rescued the survivors on August 8.

Kennedy's saga brought him to the attention of the national public for the first time. He proudly used his PT boat service record in all of his campaigns, including in his successful 1960 presidential run. Liebenow accompanied Kennedy on several campaign tours, and as president, Kennedy met with Biuku Gasa.

Woonsocket's Mills Produce Uniforms, Fake Rubber Tanks and More for the War Effort

By Norman Desmarais

While the most direct way to contribute to the war effort was to enlist in the army, navy, marines or coast guard, not everyone could or did. Those who worked in the many mills and other factories in Rhode Island producing military equipment and other war materiel also substantially contributed to the war effort. In the end, the United States far outproduced its enemies.

During World War II, Woonsocket took an active role in three of the most important industries in the state: textiles, rubber and machine tools. Taken as a whole, Woonsocket's military production was remarkable. Its factories and their workers serve as a microcosm of the industrial communities in the state that mobilized to support the war effort.

Many in Woonsocket depended, either directly or indirectly, on textile mills and other factories for their livelihood, yet prior to the war, numerous of the city's mills had closed or were on the verge of closing. In 1941, war orders started pouring in, finally putting Woonsocket on the road to recovery from the Great Depression, which had afflicted the workforce since 1929, and from other causes, such as mismanagement, competition from non-unionized mills in the South and labor problems.

The Nyanza Mill on Singleton Street in Woonsocket, as an example, was shuttered, and by January 1940, its Fall River owners had scheduled it for demolition. The mill, with 457,000 square feet of workspace valued at more than $1 million, was once the country's largest manufacturer of woolen knitted fabrics. The roof alone covered two acres. The mill had employed large numbers of area residents during World War I.

In February 1940, Governor William H. Vanderbilt and the Rhode Island Industrial Commission induced the owners to delay demolition. On March 15, the Woonsocket Lions Club and the Kiwanis Club banded together and organized a fundraiser to save Nyanza, attended by more than 1,000 people. Later in the month, 150 workers conducted a campaign that found 1,800 investors who raised $50,100—equivalent to $880,500 today.

Still, progress in saving Nyanza was falling short—the amount raised by investors was enough to purchase the mill but not to operate it. In November 1940, foreclosure seemed imminent. War orders spared the mill. In 1942, it was sold to Harry Jawitz of New York for $42,500; two years later, he sold it for $80,500.

The Goodyear Fabrics Corporation, a New Bedford subsidiary of the huge Goodyear Rubber Company of Akron, Ohio, leased the building for $30,000 a year. It obtained an important military contract to manufacture "urgently needed equipment for the armed services." At first, it ran a single shift for an eight-hour day, six days a week, employing 838 workers operating its sixty thousand spindles. A second shift started on September 18, 1944. At war's end, on August 17, 1945, Goodyear shut the plant, releasing the last 350 workers.

It did not take long for Woonsocket's other manufacturing plants to gear up for war production. Woonsocket's American Wringer Company, a major manufacturer of washing machines, had to cease manufacturing them with the outbreak of war. Records indicate that, having already been engaged on a government ordnance order, it received another military order for $1,256,000. In 1943, an Iowa newspaper reported, somehow escaping wartime censors, that American Wringer assembled landing craft for amphibious operations at Woonsocket from parts assembled by its Iowa affiliate.

The American Oerlikon-Gazda Corporation (later the A. O. G. Corporation) of Providence had a $26,800,000 contract for the manufacture of 20-millimeter antiaircraft guns for the U.S. Navy in 1941 and was negotiating for a new contract exceeding that amount. At one point early during the war, most navy ships carried this antiaircraft gun, from PT boats to aircraft carriers, as did many merchant marine vessels.

Parts of the gun were manufactured, under subcontract, by Taft-Peirce Manufacturing Company and other plants in and near Providence. Taft-Peirce, which began as the Wardwell Sewing Machine Company in

Woonsocket, established a special division to manufacture the gun's vital breech casing and handgrip. It was considered one of the war's most difficult machining jobs. It consisted of a single piece requiring some 250 separate machining operations, many of them to tolerances of four ten-thousandths of an inch (0.0004). The original forging weighed 168 pounds, and the finished piece was 42 pounds. Because the cutting and grinding process heated the metal, causing it to expand, it needed to be cooled frequently.

Taft-Peirce employed 325 people, with 40 to 45 percent of them working on the Oerlikon contract. The company added more manufacturing capacity to manufacture Adel precision valves for the U.S. Army Air Corps, radar equipment and torpedo parts for the navy and other military items.

Taft-Peirce peaked with over two thousand employees on its payroll at its Pond-East School Street complex. Company president Frederick S. Blackall, Jr. recalled that the Federal Bureau of Investigation ordered that all new employees be fingerprinted and that no one be admitted into the facility without a badge.

Taft-Peirce's Pond East School Street plant won its first Army-Navy "E" Award for excellence in war production on April 9, 1943. The pennant had a capital E within a yellow wreath of oak and laurel leaves on a vertical divided blue and red background. ARMY was on the red background and NAVY on the blue background. The award was given to the plant, not the company. A U.S. Army or Navy officer usually presented the pennant at a ceremony attended by all the employees involved in production. After the award of the pennant to the plant, the employees present received individual pins.

Nationwide, only about 5 percent of the more than eighty-five thousand companies involved in producing materials for the war effort earned the Army-Navy E Award. Taft-Peirce received five such awards, with four white stars added at successive six-month intervals for continued excellence in war production. (For a list of Rhode Island companies that won Army-Navy E Awards, see appendix A.)

Perhaps in recognition of Taft-Peirce's high-quality work, its president, Frederick Blackall, in November 1944 was selected by 1,200 New England business leaders to serve as the president of the New England Council. The council, an organization of business leaders, the six New England governors and commanding officers of the armed forces in New England, helped to coordinate war production.

Jacob Finkelstein & Sons, another Woonsocket manufacturer, was the first New England garment manufacturer to receive the Army-Navy E

Award. With the outbreak of war, the company completely retooled and obtained contracts to manufacture military outerwear—trench coats, field jackets, peacoats, leather bomber jackets and rubberized rainwear. The company's first government contract came with instructions for how to cut the material. Finkelstein requested the pattern and reworked it. After the company fulfilled the contract, it returned more than 2,000 yards of unused wool, pleasing the quartermaster general and ensuring future contracts.

Jacob Finkelstein & Sons, by being awarded five Army-Navy excellence awards, became a member of the elite 5 E club. The company proudly flew the banner above its mill for the next twenty-five years. When the father and founder, Jacob, died in 1933, his eldest son, Noah, took over the business and worked with his brothers Robert and Elliot. Meanwhile, their brother Harold served as a first lieutenant in the army. The company's Samoset Mill employed more than five hundred workers during the war.

The Uxbridge Worsted Company, headquartered in Uxbridge, Massachusetts, received the Army-Navy E Award for making uniform cloth, army and navy overcoats, shirts, bomber lining cloth, elastique and target cloth. Three of the company's eleven mills were located in Rhode Island, including the Glenark Mill in Woonsocket.

Most Woonsocket factory workers were employed in textile mills. Even before the Pearl Harbor attack, with President Franklin D. Roosevelt attempting to increase the nation's wartime readiness, the city's many textile mills joined the war production force.

On July 1, 1941, the army awarded contracts to ten Rhode Island mills to furnish 1,726,000 yards of worsted uniform cloth, with a value of $5,965,685. Impressively, this was more than 10 percent of total awards nationwide. Woonsocket mills were awarded at least five contracts.

On October 6, 1941, the army awarded Rhode Island woolen and worsted mills more contracts for 11,810,683 yards of uniform material for $3,595,395. Government contracts for woolen army cloth orders in November 1941 totaled over $10 million.

On December 7, 1941, the day Pearl Harbor was attacked, the army awarded $28,199,909 in contracts to produce 8.5 million yards of overcoat material and 3.5 million yards of lining cloth, the greatest volume of business the textile industry had received in a lump amount since World War I. Woonsocket's mills obtained a good share of these contracts as well.

The war provided a last burst of glory for the city's textile mills and put many Woonsocket families back on a solid footing after suffering through

Robert Finkelstein (*left*) and Governor J. Howard McGrath (*right*) display an "E" pennant awarded to Jacob Finkelstein & Sons, circa 1944, that would fly from the flagstaff atop its plant. *Collection of Richard Elliott Finkelstein.*

the Great Depression. (For a list of some of the Woonsocket mills, their workforces and their cloth contracts, see appendix B.)

The military placed such heavy demands upon Rhode Island's mills that little capacity was left for civilian production. Natural fibers, such as cotton, wool and linen, were in short supply. Synthetic fibers, such as nylon, polyester and rayon, were used as substitutes.

A desperate need arose for rubber tires for the war effort. There were five types of basic synthetic rubber produced in the country during the war: Buna-S, Buna-N, Butyl, neoprene and thiokol. These were converted into some five thousand compounds used in the production of rubber goods. Through ingenious compounding, manufacturers were able to produce substitutes for natural rubbers with a wide range of physical characteristics. Some were well adapted to belting, hose, packing, linings and other industrial uses and promised to continue substituting for natural rubber after the war. Some mills switched from manufacturing textiles to working with rubber and other substances.

The Alice Mill, originally built in 1889 in Fairmount, had been the largest rubber factory in the world, employing 1,500 workers. Closed since 1932, it reopened in 1941 as a subsidiary of the United States Rubber Company. The United States Rubber Company received a government contract to manufacture balloons and rubber boats for ship convoys. The factory also made inflatable rubber rafts, invasion boats, barrage balloons, lifesaving suits and wading suits for launching, repairing and maintaining

Women performed important war services by working in factories producing military equipment and supplies. Here women produce military medals, probably at a Gorham Manufacturing Company factory in Providence. *War Department short film on R.I. wartime industry, courtesy of BuyOut Footage.*

seaplanes. It operated twenty-four hours a day and even leased two floors at 162 Main Street in Woonsocket in March 1944.

The Alice Mill played a key role in an amazing campaign to deceive the German military. Allied forces deployed a number of rubber aircraft and landing craft around British airfields to trick the Germans into thinking the invasion of France would occur at Pas de Calais, the closest point to England. For the real D-Day invasion at Normandy, the Alice Mill produced rubber attack boats, wading suits and lifesaving jackets.

Alice Mill also made rubber tanks that were used by General George S. Patton's army as decoys during the latter part of the war. They were effective in drawing enemy attention and relieved some of the pressure from frontline troops.

The "Ghost Army" consisted of 1,100 men, including designer Bill Blass, who worked on camouflage. They simulated a force of 30,000. In addition to the tanks, the unit had inflatable tank transports, jeeps, halftracks, aircraft, artillery and all sorts of support vehicles. Bulldozers created tank tracks on the ground near the fakes.

One of the problems to be solved was that in the predawn hours the temperatures dropped and the air inside the inflatables condensed, causing the tank "guns" to droop. Fake radio traffic and recorded engine sounds, blasted out of five-hundred-pound speakers, supported the illusion.

The "Ghost Army" even drew friendly fire. On one occasion, there was a large gap in the center of the American line. Both the right and the left divisions knew there were no Americans deployed in that area, so when they saw tanks, they assumed them to be German and opened fire.

As the inflatable tank was top-secret, different plants worked on various stages of production. One company built four-inch-diameter tubes, another company formed the tubes into a framework and yet another company covered the frames in rubberized canvas. The rubber tanks were finally glued together in Woonsocket, where the workers were told they were making targets to train American gunners. A fake Sherman tank weighed about ninety-three pounds and could be rolled up and put in a large duffel bag.

Workers at Alice Mill were told they were making decoys and to be quiet about it. "It was decoys. End of conversation," worker Dorothy Linton recalled. Del Gariepy remembered that mill workers felt good about making products for the war effort. "So many people had their own relatives in the war that they felt they were helping," he said.

Textile manufacturing had traditionally been dominated by women workers, but during the war they filled positions at better-paying rubber and machine tool plants as well. The pay for men and women often differed. At Alice Mill, men made $38.00 for a forty-eight-to-fifty-hour work week, or about $0.79 per hour, while women earned $0.49 per hour.

To compensate for supply shortages, the nation went on a national recycling program to collect rags, paper and unwanted clothing to break down into fibers that could be used to produce new fabric. Metal was also collected and recycled into military equipment. Mills vied with one another for the honor of being the largest contributors. Results were regularly published in the newspapers. Monthly figures released by the War Production Board in Washington, D.C., showed that Rhode Island usually exceeded its quota and, impressively, led all New England states in the scrap and steel drives (finishing sixth in the nation in 1943).

The Woonsocket Retail Trade Board sponsored a war bond sale in June 1943 to raise money to pay for a B-17 "Flying Fortress" bomber to be named the *Spirit of Woonsocket*. The five-week campaign exceeded the goal of $500,000 by $68,202. A single concert by Woonsocket native Eileen

Farrell raised $151,000. The city's factory workers and owners, flush with money from military contracts, were generous with it. When former mayor J. Hector Paquin announced the honor in November 1943, he was notified by the U.S. Army Air Corps that the *Spirit of Woonsocket* was already in action at an "undisclosed front."

More Stories from Westerly, Charlestown, Jamestown, Newport, Little Compton, Providence and Pawtucket

By Christian McBurney

WESTERLY NEWSPAPER IS NATION'S FIRST TO REPORT PEARL HARBOR ATTACK

Westerly's longtime daily newspaper, the *Westerly Sun*, was the nation's first newspaper to announce the Sunday, December 7, 1941 attack on Pearl Harbor. The reason: it was the country's only newspaper to run a Sunday afternoon edition. George H. Utter, the *Sun*'s founder and first publisher, was a Seventh-day Baptist who considered Saturday the Sabbath. So he did not print a Saturday edition and instead began the family tradition of publishing a Sunday afternoon edition.

On December 7, 1941, George ("Ben") Utter, the founder's son, was the newspaper's editor and publisher. His wife, Katherine, after listening at home to one of the first radio reports of the raid, immediately called the newsroom. Ben halted production, just before the afternoon edition was printed. City editor C. Starr Baker quickly confirmed the story with the Associated Press. From the little information he gleaned, he inserted six sentences to the afternoon edition's front page. He added two sentences of his own, including that "a number of Westerly boys" were stationed in Hawaii and the Philippines.

The front page of the *Westerly Sun*, Sunday afternoon edition, December 7, 1941. Westerly Sun, *microfilm*, *Westerly Public Library*.

The production staff employed an ultra-large typeface to create the banner headline composed by Baker: "Japs Attack Hawaii and The Philippines." (While offensive today, the term "Japs" was commonly used in newspapers at the time.) The skimpy eight-sentence news report was printed in twenty-four-point type, a size normally used only for headlines. But there was one problem: the typesetting machine had only two no. 2s in twenty-four-point type. So while the White House announced the attack at 2:22 p.m., the *Sun* reported it as 2:23 p.m. Claude Maine, the composing room foreman, recalled that the type problem could have been fixed in five minutes, but no one wanted to spend that much time. The revised edition began rolling off the presses just after 3:00 p.m.

Maine remembered his feelings as he worked. "You just couldn't believe it," he said to a *Sun* interviewer years later. "Here we are a powerful country and Japan stabbed us in the back." But at the same time, he knew he was part of history. "I realized right away, this is Sunday and nobody else is printing," he recalled. "I feel as though we brought this story to the general public. I always felt proud the paper was first."

The *Sun* was the first newspaper to announce the Pearl Harbor attack due to fortunate timing and its fast work and because other newspapers that day had to run special editions.

A Navy Recruit at the Newport Naval Training Station Hears of Pearl Harbor

Howard Ziemer rose to the rank of lieutenant commander in the navy, but he started out as a training recruit in Newport. He recalled the following from early winter 1941:

> Then it was off on a bus to boot camp at Naval Training Station, Newport, RI.…We received the regulation all equalizing haircut, numerous medical shots, were issued uniforms and bedding, which included a hammock.… We were then formed into a company to begin training under the tutelage of a Chief Petty Officer. We were quarantined for the first three weeks as a precaution against various diseases. After the first three weeks of basic training, which included lots of marching, inspections, naval orientation courses and physical fitness exercises, we were granted liberty Saturday and Sunday afternoons in Newport. It was there on Sunday, December 7, we

heard of the Japanese attack on Pearl Harbor. Liberty was canceled and we were immediately recalled.

The next day we listened to the President ask Congress for a "state of war" to be declared against Japan. We all cheered. Chaos erupted throughout the reining command. Recruits by the thousands started to arrive on a base already quite full. Quonset huts appeared like magic overnight and steps were taken to move some of us out early. Rumors were rampant. At one time we were ordered into the basement of a building. This was to serve as an air raid shelter. Immediately, it was rumored New York was being bombed.

Rumors of enemy bombers headed for Rhode Island or New York turned out to be false (see chapter 1, volume 1).

HEROES SAVE NAVY FLIERS WHO CRASHED

While the vast bulk of incredible acts of courage and bravery occurred in the war zones, a few occurred within Rhode Island. Not surprisingly, they involved rescuing pilots who had crashed their planes, an all-too-common occurrence.

On December 5, 1943, a navy plane with two men aboard crashed in the West Passage about a mile to the north of Beavertail Lighthouse. Seaman First Class Clayton Albert Wood of White River Junction, Vermont, witnessed the crash. He ran on foot along the shoreline for a mile and, without resting, dove into the icy water and swam out one hundred yards out to the wreck. He then rescued the pilot, taking him to the shore. Wood plunged back into the icy water and swam one hundred yards more to rescue the second airman and assisted him to shore. Wood was awarded the Navy and Marine Corps Medal, the highest noncombat decoration awarded for heroism by the navy.

In one instance, citizens showed extraordinary bravery. On October 24, 1943, a Grumman TBF-1 Avenger piloted by Ensign Ralph E. Sethness, age twenty-eight, approached Westerly's Naval Auxiliary Air Facility (today's Westerly State Airport). The pilot's plane developed engine trouble and crashed south of the airport on the golf course near the seventh hole of the Winnapaug Country Club (still located on Shore Road). Two local young men, Robert C. Gentile and Benjamin B. York, saw the plane was in trouble and probably heard the crash. They jumped into a car and rushed to the scene, where they found the badly injured pilot lying next to the burning wreck. Live ammunition from the plane's machine guns started to explode. Disregarding their own safety, Gentile and York carried Ensign Sethness fifty feet away and laid him down. No sooner had they done so when the plane's fuel tanks exploded, spraying flaming gasoline all about the area. As the flames set off more machine gun rounds, Gentile used his body to shield the injured pilot. After two minutes, the heat of the flames forced Gentile and York to move Sethness another fifty feet away. There the two Westerly civilians tended to the injured pilot as best they could until fire and rescue units arrived. Sethness suffered a few broken bones and second-degree burns, but he recovered. A navy captain at Quonset Point commended Gentile and York, writing that their actions "undoubtedly saved the life of the pilot." Gentile and York were later awarded the Carnegie Medal of Heroism.

Not all courageous rescue attempts were successful. In winter 1944, Robert Andrew Meikle, a member of a navy rescue party, arrived at the scene after a plane at Charlestown's Naval Auxiliary Air Facility had crashed on takeoff and slid off the runway into five feet of water. The plane had turned upside down, trapping the pilot. Meikle plunged into the frigid water, swam to the aircraft and dived underwater. He tried to extricate the pilot, but his efforts were in vain, as the cockpit was embedded in several feet of mud. The pilot died. (He was probably twenty-three-year-old James Gilmore Canning of Washington, D.C., who drowned at Charlestown on February 16, 1944.) Still, Meikle was awarded the Navy and Marine Corps Medal. His citation read, "Meikle's courageous and instinctive action as a result of which he suffered acute shock and exposure which required hospitalization was in keeping with the highest traditions of the United States Naval Service."

Sometimes plane crews rescued themselves. For example, on April 6, 1945, at 10:00 p.m., a TBF Avenger torpedo plane experienced engine trouble eight miles off Martha's Vineyard. The pilot, Ensign Robert Hammer of Chicago, Illinois, was forced to make a rough sea landing traveling at a speed of eighty knots. Little time remained for the three-man crew to depart their plane, as it would sink in less than one minute. One crew member, Joel L. Stallings, quickly escaped out of the plane and began inflating a rubber life raft on the plane's port wing. Ensign Hammer also speedily climbed from the cockpit to the plane's port wing. But he noticed that the last crewman, radioman Frederick Lang, was semiconscious and unable to extricate himself from the sinking plane. Hammer dived into the thirty-six-degree water and tried to force open Lang's submerged escape hatch. He failed. After coming up for air, he plunged in again and this time succeeded. He then grasped Lang by his parachute harness, braced his feet against the side of the plane and pulled Lang out of the hatch, just as the plane disappeared underwater. After inflating the unconscious radioman's lifejacket, Hammer towed him to the raft. Hammer and Stallings got Lang aboard the life raft. Hammer and Stallings then rowed their small life raft for six and a half hours before finally landing near Oak Bluff on Martha's Vineyard. They found an abandoned house, where they started a fire for warmth, and all three were rescued a short time later. Hammer was awarded the Navy and Marine Corps Medal for saving his fellow crewman. It should also be noted that the training Hammer and Stallings would have received at the swimming pool at Quonset Point Naval Air Station, including inflating rafts, inflating a victim's lifejacket and getting a victim into a floating life raft, served them well.

Fort Church at Little Compton Evolves into a Major Fortification

Even before U.S. entry into World War II, construction began on Fort Church, at the tip of Little Compton. When fully developed during the war, the army coastal fortifications consisted of three separate "reservations" encompassing a total of more than 230 acres and hosting some four hundred soldiers. Fort Church Military Reservation protected the eastern entrance of Narragansett Bay, while on the other side of the bay, Fort Varnum and Fort Greene in Narragansett and Fort Burnside at Beavertail Point on Jamestown protected the western entrances to the bay.

Fort Church's West Reservation, off West Main Road and bordered to the west by the Sakonnet River, covered 140 acres. It contained Battery Gray, a large underground concrete bunker complex that was topped with tons of dirt and grass. Battery Gray hosted two massive 16-inch cannon spaced 500 feet apart. Designed to be installed on battleships, the artillery pieces had a range of 26 miles and covered the area from the tip of Martha's Vineyard to the eastern side of Block Island. In summer 1941, the two 16-inch cannons were delivered by train from Springfield, Massachusetts, to the Tiverton depot, with each one loaded onto a huge flatbed truck. They were hauled down to Little Compton at a snail's pace, two miles per hour, requiring two days to complete the journey to

Fort Church. Avis Lawton recalled the crowds lining the procession. "I remember them watching them go by Taylor's Lane. Everyone was just waiting for the road to cave in," she said, but it never did.

While the 16-inch guns were never fired at an enemy, they were occasionally fired during practice drills. To fire a single two-thousand-pound projectile required one thousand pounds of gunpowder and cost the War Department $3,000 (in today's dollars, about $45,000).

Ted Bowen, eleven years old at the time, recalled that his family—whose home stood on Warren Point, directly under the guns' line of fire to the north—was given advance notice. He said, "We were told to open our windows and secure our china to avoid damage from the concussive effects of the blast." He added, "The fire power of the guns was awesome. You could feel the projectile go overhead. You'd sense the nearness of the shell several seconds before you'd hear the tremendous report of the firing—then coming back, the echo." The West Reservation also hosted a plotting room, gymnasium, recreation hall, pistol range and rifle range.

According to a *Providence Journal* article in 1946, the casemates with the appearance of grass-covered hills "offer protection from poison gas, aerial bombardment and shell attacks. Housed in well-ventilated underground compartments are power plants sufficient in capacity to supply a municipality with electric power, extensive magazines and auxiliary equipment."

Across West Main Road from the West Reservation was the East Reservation, the home of Battery Reilly, which like Battery Gray had a massive subterranean concrete complex that bulged above ground and was camouflaged to look like a grassy hill. Battery Reilly, encompassing seventy-four acres, contained two 8-inch cannons. The East Reservation also hosted most of the soldiers and had at least nine barracks, a mess hall, officers' quarters, a store and even a movie theater. While civilian access to the West Reservation was strictly limited, occasionally civilians were able to get into the East Reservation—some local children saw their first movies there.

The South Reservation, at Warren Point, covered twenty-one acres and had a battery consisting of two 6-inch cannon overlooking Rhode Island Sound. They had a range of sixteen miles and a projectile weighing more than one hundred pounds.

While the smaller guns—8-inchers, 6-inchers and 155-millimeter howitzers—had shorter ranges than the 16-inch cannon, they could fire at more rapid rates at high speed enemy targets. The 16-inch guns were

One of two 8-inch guns placed at Battery Reilly at Fort Church in Little Compton, circa 1942. *Dugan Family Collection, Fort Adams Trust.*

intended to counter enemy battleships carrying similar guns, while the 8-inch and 6-inch guns could contend with cruisers and lighter ships. Each reservation also had fire-control concrete structures designed to look like farmhouses that included dummy chimneys and windows painted on the concrete walls. Beginning in 1943, one contained a SCR 296-A radar system used to guide the long guns.

Fort Church's expansion created some tensions in Little Compton. The reservations were acquired largely by eminent domain, including one house and property that the Wilbour family had owned for more than two hundred years. Some townspeople questioned whether the German threat justified the enormous expense of Fort Church's fortifications. Navy brass in Washington, D.C., might have agreed with that assessment. But they were concerned that if Germany ever did attack the U.S. coast, the outraged reaction of the American public might lead to a significant diversion of crucial resources from the European theater of war to the American homeland.

HARRY TRUMAN CAMPAIGNS IN PROVIDENCE AND PAWTUCKET

During the war, Harry S. Truman visited Rhode Island for a single day. Roosevelt selected the U.S. senator from Missouri to be his running mate in the presidential campaign of 1944, and he was nominated as the Democratic candidate for vice president.

On October 30, 1944, on a campaign swing through southeastern New England, Truman arrived at Providence. He was entertained at a luncheon for fifty special guests in the Narragansett Hotel and later visited the state capitol to shake hands with state employees. Rhode Island wartime governor J. Howard McGrath then gave Truman a tour of the massive Providence Shipyard, where they saw workers busily building Liberty ships and combat-loaded cargo vessels for the navy.

At a news conference afterward, Truman predicted "a landslide" victory for Roosevelt on Election Day, November 7. Truman expressed his view that "a whispering campaign about President Roosevelt's health" had made no impression on the voters and that such efforts to discredit the chief executive would never amount to anything except to "backfire on those who started them."

Truman traveled north to McCoy Stadium in Pawtucket, often used for sporting events, to speak at a rally before enthusiastic Democrat supporters. Urging voters to give the president an unprecedented fourth term, he used a sports analogy, declaring it "always poor policy to send in substitutes when you have a winning team on the field." He added, "You cannot take a chance on inexperienced leadership in the midst of a great war when the lives of our fighting men and the future of the nation are at stake." After

Vice presidential candidate Harry S. Truman (*far left*) and Governor J. Howard McGrath (*far right*) on their way to tour Providence Shipyard, October 30, 1944. *Andresen, Providence Shipyard.*

the speech, the candidate returned to Providence to board his special train car for a trip to New York City to give another speech at a rally at Madison Square Garden.

Eight days later, the nation's voters elected Roosevelt to his fourth term. Five months after that, Roosevelt died of heart failure and Truman became president. In September 1945, Truman appointed McGrath his solicitor general.

7

George H.W. Bush Trains at Charlestown, November 1943 to January 1944

By Christian McBurney

On his eighteenth birthday, June 12, 1942, future U.S. president George H.W. Bush enlisted in the navy. After completing a ten-month course on naval aviation, he was commissioned as an ensign in the U.S. Naval Reserve on June 9, 1943, several days before his nineteenth birthday, making him the navy's youngest pilot at that time.

Bush was assigned as a bomber and aerial photography pilot on a TBF-1 Avenger torpedo and dive-bomber on the newly built aircraft carrier USS *San Jacinto*. He was part of Torpedo Squadron VT-51. The TBF Avenger was not the fastest plane in the sky, but it was sturdy, reliable and the largest single-engine carrier-based plane used in World War II.

VT-51 trained for several weeks at the rudimentary Naval Auxiliary Air Facility at Hyannis, Massachusetts. Bush and the squadron's other Avenger pilots often flew to Narragansett Bay to practice dropping torpedoes, using an abandoned lightship for a target.

Bush and the rest of VT-51 ended up at the Naval Auxiliary Air Facility (NAAF) at Charlestown, Rhode Island, for their final training on land before assignment to the carrier and on to the Pacific. Bush arrived at Charlestown on Thanksgiving Day, November 30, 1943.

While at Charlestown, Bush wrote six letters to his mother, Dorothy Walker Bush, at Greenwich, Connecticut. Bush was close to his mother,

Naval Aviator Cadet George H.W. Bush, early 1942. *George H.W. Bush Library and Museum.*

who once visited him at the Charlestown facility—apparently the only mother of a VT-51 pilot to do so. Only one letter to his fiancée, Barbara Pierce, then a student at Smith College, has survived. While he could not describe in detail what he was doing, because of security concerns, his letters provide the best description of a pilot's life at the Charlestown field at this stage of the war. Unlike so many other wartime letter writers, Bush showed his feelings in his letters, including his love for Barbara, his determination to succeed as a naval aviator and his understandable fear of crashing his airplane.

NAAF Charlestown made a favorable first impression on Bush. "We live in a nice B.O.Q. [Bachelor Officer Quarters] with two-man rooms, furnished with comfortable furniture," he wrote his mother. He added, "The base is quite small, but the field, in keeping with Navy tradition, [has] lovely long runways and other excellent facilities." On time off, Bush continued, Charlestown "is a small town and everyone goes to Westerly instead," for restaurants and movies.

Bush and his fellow pilots had to master takeoffs and landings on land at Charlestown before they could try them on their carrier at sea. Bush never mentioned the catapult and arresting gear system employed at Charlestown to simulate carrier takeoffs and landings, but he must have used it. Gunnery and bombing skills would have been honed using the pilots' .30- and .50-caliber machine guns, 20-millimeter cannon and several types of practice bombs on various coastal, island and bay targets.

On December 9, Bush informed his mother that his squadron captain had assigned him a new TBF-1 Avenger. Since it was his second plane and he named his planes after his fiancée, he named it *Barbara II*. It was a busy day for the young pilot: "Today we had a good deal of flying and two hours work tonight. The night was beautiful and I really enjoyed it."

As an aerial photographer officer, a camera had to be installed on Bush's Avenger. On December 10, he flew it up to Naval Air Station Quonset Point to have the camera installed and then returned to Charlestown for more training, using other planes. Bush wrote to Barbara on December 12, "The wind of late has been blowing like mad and our flying has been cut to a minimum."

Bush's December 12 letter to Barbara is an extraordinary one that rivals the best wartime love letters, revealing both the deep affection he held for the special woman in his life and his duty to serve his country. George first mentioned how thrilled he was that their engagement had been announced in that day's edition of the *New York Herald Tribune*. Bush wrote to Barbara, "[I]t should be simple for me to tell you how desperately happy I was to open the papers and see the announcement of our engagement, but somehow I can't possibly say all in a letter. I should like to." He continued: "I love you, precious, with all my heart and to know that you love me means my life. How often I have thought about this immeasurable joy that will be ours someday. How lucky our children will be to have a mother like you."

Bush then addressed the tension he felt between his powerful yearning to be with his fiancée (whom he nicknamed Bar) and the strong duty he felt to serve overseas at this crucial time in the country's history:

> *As the days go by the time of our departure* [to the war zone] *draws nearer. For a long time I had anxiously looked forward to the day when we would go aboard and set to sea. It seemed that obtaining that goal would be all I could desire for some time, but, Bar, you have changed all that. I cannot say that I do not want to go—for that would be a lie. We have been working for a long time with a single purpose in mind, to be so equipped that we could meet and defeat our enemy. I do want to go because it is my part....Even now, with a good while between us and the sea, I am thinking of getting back. This may sound melodramatic, but if it does it is only my inadequacy to say what I mean. Bar, you have made my life full of everything I could even dream of—my complete happiness should be* [my] *token of my love for you.*

On December 15, Bush and the rest of VT-51 was invited to Camden, New Jersey, to attend the commissioning ceremonies of their aircraft carrier, USS *San Jacinto*. Bush invited both Barbara and his mother to attend. Just before the ceremony started, George thrilled Barbara by giving her an engagement ring.

Bush enjoyed leave at Christmastime, staying with his family at Greenwich and seeing Barbara as much as he could. He returned to Charlestown on December 29. He sat down and wrote to his mother, "Had a marvelous time and back to the grind." The lovesick pilot added, "It was such fun being with [Barbara] for all that time, but awful hard to leave. Oh how I wish we were married. Perhaps in a year we will be able to get married. That's a long way off and a lot can happen though." In most of his letters, Bush expressed his longing to be with his fiancée.

On his return, Bush began flying at nighttime. This training was considered essential, as Japanese pilots often attacked at night. But night flying was dangerous, as airplanes then had no radar or other instruments to facilitate flying at night. (Bush was not part of the night fighter teams that used radar developed at Spraycliff Observatory at Jamestown; they would arrive at Charlestown after his departure.) Bush wrote, "We are now operating on a noon to noon schedule and the only thing we do get is a good long sleep. We live on a two meal and sometimes one meal day but sleep will make up for it." Bush flew at night, sometimes until 2:00 a.m. He worried his mother about one trip: "At first I felt most miserable up there cause I was so tired but it got better as time went on and the evening was uneventful." In another letter to his mother, he revealed his awareness of the dangers of night training, remarking, "no night flying thank heavens."

Bush's immediate commander, Lieutenant Commander Donald Melvin, a seasoned naval aviator, kept Bush busy flying on New Year's Eve, leaving no time for the lanky pilot to visit his Greenwich home. Bush and his fellow pilots did nothing special on New Year's Eve. They preferred to skip a party that night in the BOQ, attended mostly by station personnel and their wives. The young pilot went to bed at 10:30 p.m. The next morning, he flew his plane to Quonset Point and returned that afternoon on a "beautiful day" for flying.

On January 2, 1944, Bush reported to his mother that "we have gotten in quite a few flying hours. Today it was most interesting." Bush could not say why. He continued, "Tomorrow we go back to our old schedule so once again I will be getting three meals a day but probably not as much sleep."

On the evening of January 2, Bush wrote, "The captain just informed us that there will be no flying tonight—away to our cars. That is such a nice feeling. You prepare yourself for a couple of hours of work—most unpleasant work at that—and then release. It's very fine." This incident shows the strain pilots were under in night training, even though Bush knew he needed it.

On January 11, Bush disclosed to his mother some difficulties he had flying his Avenger that day. "The cold weather seems to make our engines temperamental and they act peculiarly causing no end of consternation especially when we are airborne and the thing starts to bang and sputter. Flying can make me awfully nervous especially navy flying since it's water all the way." "We have had two major accidents lately," Bush added, no doubt

As with other pilots flying TBF Avengers at Charlestown and Quonset Point, George H.W. Bush practiced dropping torpedoes in Narragansett Bay. *Naval War College Museum.*

increasing his mother's anxiety level. Bush expressed his preference for flying over land, where a safe landing could more likely be made. Realizing the effect this letter might have on its recipient, he said comfortingly, "Don't get the idea that I'm…worrying myself sick, cause I'm not, but every now and then I have an uneasy moment or two."

Bush was right to be concerned about flying over frigid water in winter. An engine failure could quickly lead to tragedy, as a pilot who operated out of NAAF Westerly in November 1944 recalled years later:

> *I witnessed the death of John S. Ketchum, a close friend. One of our first flights was to go out over the ocean and get back up to speed in daytime gunnery. Ketchum's engine failed and he had to make a water landing. We circled over him, noting that he got out okay. The water was so terribly cold that he likely could not even inflate his life jacket. Shortly after he disappeared below the waves. Oh, if we only had been able to help him.….About 5 minutes is the longest one can survive in the ocean at those*

temperatures. All we could do was circle overhead, finally departing for the flight back to the base. That was a sad experience, but one to be repeated in the months ahead in the Pacific.

Bush concluded his January 11 letter, "Tomorrow I am going to Quonset and then up to [NAAF Hyannis] on a photo mission preceding a sham attack" on a squadron based there. "We fly up there in Cape Cod Bay every day"—an interesting tidbit about pilot training at Charlestown.

San Jacinto was undergoing work at Philadelphia. On January 12, Bush was ordered to fly his Avenger to Philadelphia to pick up his squadron captain and another officer. On his way, Bush flew low over his parents' house in Greenwich, but to his disappointment, he "saw no cars or anything." He remained overnight in Philadelphia, going to a nice restaurant in the evening and sleeping onboard *San Jacinto* at night. "It is quite nice aboard the ship," he noted. It was small for a carrier, capable of carrying about forty-three planes.

Bush's training program at Charlestown was nearing its end, but not before a harrowing incident occurred on one of his flights. In a January 18 letter, Bush informed his mother that the day's flight at first was good: "We stayed here [at Charlestown] and made a torpedo attack with the whole air group. It is a comforting feeling having those fighters for cover." Then he continued:

On the actual run-in, I had considerable difficulty. My [rear] escape hatch blew off and knocked a big hole in the tail. We were going real fast and I was a bit anxious as I didn't know how much strain the tail could take. Not only that but the middle cockpit hatch also blew open and my own was almost forced out. All in all it was a very confused deal and I was glad to get home.

Fortunately, the mishaps did not result in a fatal accident for the future president.

Bush looked back on his flight training with satisfaction: "Our training syllabus is over and we are lucky to have had all the hours we did. Some navy guys go into combat with 250 hours, whereas right now I have 550." The young pilot told his mother of the building excitement in his squadron about the pending shakedown cruise on *San Jacinto* and their assignment to the Pacific theater.

Bush probably departed Charlestown on January 21. He arrived at Norfolk, Virginia, on January 23. *San Jacinto* would arrive there, and the squadron would begin training from the ship. In a letter written that day,

Bush revealed to this mother, "I was distressed over the news of Harry Synow. Before this trip I didn't quite see how all the accidents occur but now I know full well. We had one which sounds very much similar to his. I'll tell you about all that later." Bush apparently was referring to a fatal airplane accident experienced by a friend at another base and also to one that may have occurred on a flight from Charlestown. From 1943 to 1945, at least forty-five pilots were killed in training accidents flying out of Charlestown. Bush had avoided that fate. During his time in Rhode Island, there were no accidental pilot deaths at Charlestown, but in December 1943 three crashes of airplanes flying out of Quonset Point killed a total of eleven pilots and other airmen.

In late January, Ensign Bush and the rest of his squadron flew their planes onto the deck of *San Jacinto* for the first time. Bush wrote to his mother and father (Prescott Bush), "We, the TBFs, landed first. The ship looked really swell steaming along in her battle camouflage. We made a few practice passes down wind and then she swung around into the wind and we came aboard. She was moving at a good clip and the air was nice and smooth, facilitating the landings. We each made 3 landings and then cut our motors on the deck." As Bush was one of the first pilots to accomplish the feat at sea, the

George H.W. Bush named TBF Avengers assigned to him for training after his fiancée Barbara. His aircraft at Charlestown was named *Barbara II*, so this photo was taken after he departed Rhode Island in January 1944. *George H.W. Bush Library and Museum.*

carrier crew showered him with congratulations. Eventually, Bush logged 116 takeoffs and landings on his carrier, with no accidents. His Charlestown training had paid off.

After its shakedown cruise, *San Jacinto* joined a fleet of navy warships operating against Marcus and Wake Islands in May 1944 and the Marianas the next month. On June 19, the fleet fought in one of the largest air battles of the war and won. Returning from his mission, Bush made a forced water landing. The destroyer, USS *Clarence K. Bronson*, rescued the crew, but the plane was lost. On July 25, Bush and another pilot received credit for sinking a small cargo ship. Bush was promoted to lieutenant, junior grade.

On August 1, *San Jacinto* commenced operations against the Japanese in the Bonin Islands. On September 2, Bush piloted one of four aircraft from VT-51 that attacked Japanese installations on the island of Chichi Jima, just six hundred miles from Tokyo. His crew included Radioman Second Class John Delaney of Providence, Rhode Island, and a volunteer gunner, Lieutenant Junior Grade William White. As they started their attack, the four TBM Avengers from VT-51 encountered intense antiaircraft fire. Bush's aircraft was hit, and his engine caught on fire. He completed his attack, releasing bombs over his target and scoring several damaging hits. With smoke filling up the cockpit, Bush flew several miles from the island and gave the order to bail out. He successfully bailed out, landing in water. One other crew member on his Avenger—either Delaney or White—jumped out of the aircraft, but his parachute did not open and he plunged to his death. Both Delaney and White were killed; their bodies were never recovered. While Bush anxiously waited for four hours in his small inflated raft and without a paddle or fresh water, several navy fighters circled protectively overhead warding off small approaching Japanese boats. Eventually, he was rescued by the lifeguard submarine USS *Finback*.

Bush returned to *San Jacinto* in November 1944 and participated in operations in the Philippines. His squadron, after suffering 50 percent casualties to its pilots, was sent back to the United States in December. Throughout 1944, Bush flew fifty-eight combat missions, for which he received the Distinguished Flying Cross and three Air Medals. He and Barbara were finally married on January 6, 1945. They remained married for seventy-three years, becoming the longest married couple in U.S. presidential history.

8

Childhood Memories of the Homefront at Quonochontaug

By Christian McBurney

Residents of Rhode Island's charming summer coastal communities put up with the homefront restrictions that other Rhode Islanders had to endure: at night the shades of their houses had to be blacked out; the top half of automobile headlights had black tape applied to them; they were subject to rationing of meat, gasoline and tires, among other items; and they had to avoid entering the many military zones in the state unless they had permission.

But unlike interior and northern communities, the southern Rhode Island coastal communities were on the front lines of the German submarine war. No one knew whether a German submarine would drop off spies or saboteurs on the beach. Residents even feared an invasion, even if one was unlikely as long as the United States and British navies controlled the North Atlantic waters.

In Rhode Island and along the rest of the East Coast, army soldiers generally patrolled open stretches of beach, while the coast guard handled more difficult coastline that needed the support of patrol vessels. Army soldiers patrolled southern Rhode Island mainland beaches, including at Quonochontaug. At nearby Camp Burlingame, in Burlingame State Park, a small mobile army force with trucks pulling artillery pieces and even a few tanks could be rushed to any threatened point. This system was in place throughout 1942 and until late 1943, when both the army and coast guard rapidly reduced their beach defense forces.

This chapter contains the recollections of residents from one of Rhode Island's mainland summer communities, Quonochontaug (known as "Quonnie"). During the war, they were children, ranging from ages eight to young teenagers. Yet their memories remain vivid.

Ted Balcezak, eleven years old in 1942, would walk down from his Quonnie cottage to meet army soldiers patrolling the beach at night. The soldiers often sat on the beach near his house for fifteen minutes before continuing on patrol. They started their patrol at the new army post at Blue Shutters and ended it at the Charlestown Breachway. They patrolled in pairs—one carried a large radio in a backpack, while the other held a lantern that had a three-inch-diameter lamp connected to a battery pack the size of a small loaf of bread. The lamp, which could signal other troops on the beach, was to be used only in emergencies. Each solder also carried a loaded rifle. The young men liked to talk with Ted, showing off their rifles and reminiscing about the lives they left behind in their distant hometowns.

The army post near Blue Shutters, at what is now 468 East Beach Road, was primarily a communications bunker with a cable connecting it to the lookout station in back of the First Baptist Church of Charlestown at Quonochontaug just north of Route 1 and to lookout stations on Block Island. Many residents thought the army post also stored ammunition, but that has not been confirmed.

Carol Waterman, about ten years old in 1942, remembered meeting patrolling soldiers. "They would let us look at their rifles and try their gas masks on," she told an interviewer in 2002. She said that bored patrolling soldiers searched for a ray of light in a house, allowing them to knock on the door of the offending house. Invariably, they would be invited in, fed and entertained, she recalled.

Bill Wholean, fourteen years old in 1942, remembered that patrolling soldiers would "hit the telephone pole and crank up the field phone" to inform headquarters of their location. Ted Balcezak did not recall that occurring on his part of the beach.

During the day on the beach, children saw evidence of the war beyond their shores. Balcezak remembered his excitement at spotting submarines breach the surface of the water and then quickly submerge. (He hoped they were not enemy submarines.) In a journal he kept, for July 1, 1943, Wholean recorded seeing about fifty ships assembling in a convoy offshore, presumably headed for Britain. Crispin Jones recalled seeing a hospital ship with a Red Cross sign on it. If foamy white lines were spotted in the distance, he knew PT boats were exercising. The sea water rolling up on the

This house at 468 East Beach Road was built over part of the remains of a communications bunker that was linked by cable to a lookout station in the building at 5075 Old Post Road behind the Baptist Church on Route 1 and a communications center on Block Island. *Norman Desmarais.*

seashore was sometimes tainted with spent fuel or spilled oil, "but we did not complain," Jones remembered.

Quonnie resident Dick Hutchins remembered army soldiers based at Camp Burlingame conducting training maneuvers on the beach. They would bring down machine guns and antiaircraft guns (probably mobile 37- or 40-millimeter guns) during the daytime. He recalled seeing a navy plane towing a canvas sleeve at the end of a long cable that army soldiers on the beach fired at with antiaircraft guns. Another time, at night from his bedroom window, he heard a plane approaching his area of the beach when suddenly a searchlight opened its beam on the plane and an antiaircraft gun fired tracers at it. (The searchlight was probably connected to radar equipment that could track the oncoming plane in the night sky.)

Charlotte Houle recalled that as a young girl, she would occasionally find washed up on the beach bottles with messages in them written in foreign languages. The messages would be turned over to army soldiers. Houle was once informed that as a result of a message she turned in, the beach patrol was doubled that night.

Several Quonnie residents recalled the destruction of the five-foot-high Fresh Pond Rock between East Beach and Central Beach. Before the war, entire families could sit on it for great photographs. In October 1942, Carol Waterman saw the army dynamite it, reducing it to rubble. No official reason was announced for blowing up the rock, but residents heard several explanations: it interfered with line of sight (Germans dropped off by a submarine could seek shelter behind it); it was too much of a landmark for passing German U-boats; and it interfered with the radar deployed at Blue Shutters. While the decision was likely based on a combination of all three factors, Waterman thought the soldiers just wanted an excuse to blow up something.

Edmund Sayer recalled that as a ten-year-old one day, probably in 1942, while walking with his younger sister in the area of East Beach heading toward the breachway, he discovered a large cube-shaped hole in the high beach, at least six feet long, six feet wide and six feet deep. Sayer remembers: "We hustled back to tell our parents. I recall my dad saying he reported it to the FBI, was himself interrogated, but never could find out what the FBI learned, if anything. We always assumed it was to store and hide something." It could simply have been U.S. Army soldiers had dug a two-man foxhole for a machine gun, but incidents like these aroused the populace.

Children could also wind up in dangerous places. Disregarding their parents' instructions, young Fredericka Bettinger and her female friend swam across the Charlestown Breachway for a picnic. They discovered the area was being used for live target practice. After they swam back, an army officer pulled up in a jeep and drove them back to Quonnie, where the girls' mothers waited for them on the beach with stern expressions.

There were rumors of German spies being dropped off by U-boats. These increased when newspapers in July 1942 announced the capture of four German saboteurs who had been dropped off by a U-boat on a beach at Amagansett, Long Island, and had carried ashore small quantities of TNT and bomb materials. Their discovery led to expanded beach patrols across the Northeast. Bill Wholean recalled that army officers asked residents to keep an eye out for rubber boats that could be left by other saboteurs. But none was found, and there were never any confirmed sightings of German spies on Rhode Island's coast.

James Mageau recalled as a young boy residing in the village of nearby Cross' Mills, "hurrying down to the corner of Old Post Road" and sitting

Fresh Pond Rock, a favorite spot for family photographs on Quonochontaug Beach for decades, was destroyed during the war by U.S. armed forces. *Quonochontaug Historical Society.*

on a stone wall next to Ben Gavitt's General Store and Grist Mill "to watch as a convoy of Army tanks and trucks pulling artillery went rolling by." He added, "Several years later I was told about how angry some local farmers became because during its field maneuvers, the Army drove its tanks and artillery through their fences, stampeding the cows, ruining their hay fields and driving over the crops."

By late 1943, with the American invasion of North Africa, the United States' war effort had turned from the defensive to the offensive. Fear of enemy attack on the beaches receded and beach patrols were reduced, including at Quonochontaug. But a new neighbor became active in June 1943 until the end of the war, the Naval Auxiliary Air Facility at Charlestown. Night fighter training (see chapter 13), conducted necessarily at nighttime, particularly disrupted locals from April 1944 to August 1945.

Ted Balcezak recalled the difficulty he had sleeping nights, given the continuous roar of airplane engines at the nearby airfield, as pilots practiced simulated aircraft carrier takeoffs and landings. Other pilots, engaged in night fighter training, zoomed over his house. "You had to get used to it to sleep," Balcezak said. During the day, some "hot dog" pilots would fly so low that he could see their faces—the pilots often waved at him or tipped their wings.

Carol Waterman also recalled pilots at Charlestown flying at night. She remembered seeing flares on the beaches, a sign that searchers were looking for a crashed plane and its pilot. Edmund Sayer mentioned seeing a navy rescue boat moored in the ocean, nearly opposite Governor's Island, ready to pick up any downed pilots. James Mageau, then residing at nearby Cross' Mills just off the beach, remembered,

> *On occasion we would be awakened in the middle of the night because our yard and house would suddenly be lit up like it was daylight outside. Loud Navy "crash" trucks with huge search lights would be searching for a Navy plane that went missing. The planes had always crashed somewhere else and we would learn later if the pilot was found dead in the wreckage, as many were.*

Quonnie residents were too far away from the gun emplacements stationed at Point Judith to the east to see or hear the firing practice of the coastal artillery. Tom Battista remembers as a seven-year-old lying on an army cot looking out of an attic window of his family's summer house at Olivo's Beach (west of Scarborough Beach) and seeing the sky lit up by cannon fire. "The many rounds shook our tiny home," Battista recalled. Another elderly man informed the author that when one of the massive 16-inch guns was test fired at Fort Greene in Narragansett, it broke windows for two or three miles around. "People were not too happy about it," he said, but "they took it as part of their sacrifice for the war effort." To the west of Quonnie, at Watch Hill, Dave Moore recalled that one summer day in 1944, he and his young friends were digging for clams off Napatree Point in an area marked off limits for military use. Suddenly navy TBF/TBM Avenger planes began using a part of the beach to practice dropping bombs—fortunately, the bombs were duds.

Seabees Test a Pontoon Airfield on Narragansett Bay

By Christian McBurney and Norman Desmarais

The Seabees are rightfully renowned for inventing at Davisville, and manufacturing at West Davisville, Quonset huts that were ubiquitous in all American theaters of war. The Seabees should be just as celebrated for developing and testing pontoons at Allen Harbor (also known as Allen's Harbor) in Davisville. Pontoons became the "ship to shore" solution for landing and supplying large forces without access to conventional harbor facilities. They were crucial to successful Allied landings in Sicily, the Normandy beaches and numerous Pacific islands.

Captain John N. Laycock of the navy's Bureau of Yards and Docks was the key innovator. He developed the idea of using hollow sheet steel watertight boxes as standard-sized pontoons and interlocking them to make structures such as docks, piers and barges. The pontoon system was perfected, first at the Pontoon Experimental Area at Quonset Point and, starting in spring 1942, at the Advance Base Proving Ground located at the northeastern edge of Davisville. An impressive pontoon staging and training area was established at Allen Harbor. In October 1942, a Pontoon School for teaching Seabees how to construct and deploy pontoon assemblies was moved to the Advance Base Proving Ground.

In its final World War II form, each pontoon was a hollow cube with ¼-inch steel for the tops and bottoms and 1/8-inch for the sides. The steel plates were welded together in a box shape and floated to test that no water would seep inside.

There were three types of pontoons: the five-by-seven-by-five standard size for universal use, a curved-bow pontoon for transport service and a wedge-box pontoon for landing use. Remarkably, each standard-sized one could carry in the water up to 4 tons. One of Captain Laycock's key innovations was to develop an interlocking system (known as "attachment jewelry") that connected the pontoons to form larger and stronger structures. A pontoon assembly six pontoons wide and eight long, the most common size used for making larger structures, could carry a 150-ton load.

Completed pontoons for use in Europe were stacked high on the wharves at the Advance Base Depot in Davisville and shipped directly to Europe. Those destined for use in the Pacific were shipped flat to one of five sites in the Pacific for final assembly.

The navy's 210-page *Pontoon Gear Manual*, revised in March 1944, listed dozens of specific assemblies approved for use following testing at the Advance Base Proving Ground. Pontoon structures were used as bridges, wharves, causeways, "rhino" ferries, barges, dry docks, pile drivers, tugboats, floating cranes and seaplane service piers and ramps. On land, they could serve as water tanks, gas tanks and bridges.

During the invasion of Sicily, pontoon causeways were crucial for rapidly unloading cargo-laden vehicles from landing craft (LSTs). Typically, two two-by-thirty pontoons were slung along either side of an LST. As the LST approached a beach, Seabees cut the pontoons loose from the sides so that they floated alongside the vessel and rode onto the beach on their own momentum. The pontoon causeways were then strung together. In an experiment at Allen Harbor, the elapsed time from casting free the pontoons to driving the first vehicles from the LST onto the causeway took just seven minutes.

The "rhino" ferry was designed for short cross-channel operations like the D-Day invasion at Normandy. It was composed of 180 interlocked standard-size pontoons, six across and thirty long, and was powered by the largest outboard engines then available. Special curved-face pontoons were placed at the bow and stern. The ferries had steering gear, a speed of about four knots, a shallower draft than landing craft, and could carry a load of 275 long tons. In August 1943, Seabees conducted key tests of rhinos at the Advance Base Proving Ground at Davisville observed by senior U.S. Navy and British Admiralty officials.

Both the Americans and the British used rhino ferries for the invasion of Europe. Over 85 percent of all vehicular equipment landed on the American beaches at Normandy in the first ten days came ashore on Seabee-piloted rhino ferries.

Seabees at the Advance Base Proving Ground at Davisville experiment with different pontoon structures, September 29, 1943. The structure with the towers is a floating dry dock. Quonset huts are to the right. *National Archives.*

In the Pacific theater, pontoons were configured as dry docks of many sizes. The standard "7-by-30" pontoon dry dock was 215 feet long and 70 feet wide, with stabilizer towers on its sides 27 feet high. Seawater was allowed to flood the pontoons to submerge the flat part of the dock, allowing a vessel to be moved over it. Then the water in the pontoons was pumped out to raise the dock. The vessel would be maneuvered to stand on keel blocks affixed to the dock. Early in the war, small dry docks serviced PT boats, but by war's end, Seabees were fabricating enormous floating dry docks capable of servicing battleships. Some dry docks were so large they had to be turned sideways to be towed through the Panama Canal.

While most of the activity at the Advance Base Proving Ground was devoted to developing and testing pontoon gear, other types of new equipment were tested, including bulldozers, engines, water treatment plants and even laundry machines. A dredging school at the site taught Seabees to deepen harbors and to use the landfill to build airfields.

In 1943, one of the war's most interesting innovations was developed at Allen Harbor: a mobile floating airfield. Codenamed Project Sock, it was inspired by British prime minister Winston Churchill. Captain Laycock once found himself in a meeting with Churchill, who expressed his interest in the feasibility of building pontoon landing fields for use in the Indian Ocean, but possibly for the D-Day invasion as well. They could also support American amphibious operations against Japanese-held islands in the Pacific Ocean.

An experimental floating airfield, called a Floating Pontoon Flight Deck, was constructed by Seabees at Allen Harbor. The floating airfield structure was 1,810 feet long and 272 feet wide. Measured another way, it was 312 pontoons long and 38 pontoons wide and used a total of 10,291 pontoons. The steel flight deck was 175 feet wide. Off to the side was a narrower parking strip that could hold at least 90 aircraft with wings folded. Connecting the

A rare photograph of the experimental Pontoon Landing Facility built by the Seabees in Davisville. The floating airfield was 1,810 by 272 feet. The landing deck on the left was 175 feet wide. The parking strip on the right could hold ninety airplanes with wings folded. Seven bridges connected the landing deck and the parking strip, with open water in between. *U.S. Navy Seabee Museum.*

In November 1943, the mobile pontoon landing deck was towed by tugboats into a cove in Narragansett Bay and was successfully tested by aircraft from Quonset Point. *National Archives.*

flight deck and parking strip were seven bridges, with open water in between the bridges. Tugboats towed the floating pontoon structure.

In November 1943, the pontoon landing field was towed into a cove in Narragansett Bay with about one hundred navy officials onboard. During testing, navy planes from Quonset Point successfully landed on it and took off from it. More intensive testing was done through January 1944. A total of 140 successful takeoffs and landings were recorded in both smooth and rough waters, including 9 at night using torch pots for deck lighting. Refueling of aircraft was conducted by gasoline trucks driven on the mobile airfield refilled from a pontoon fuel barge. The pontoon airfield had some advantages over aircraft carriers: no arresting gear was needed or used for landings, and takeoffs and landings could be executed at shorter intervals.

Bombing tests were conducted in Narragansett Bay. It was determined that damage from four one-hundred-pound bombs exploding on the floating deck did not interfere with flight operations and could be easily repaired.

It was estimated that the disassembled parts of the floating deck could be carried in the holds of eight Liberty ships. Upon arriving at the designated location, eight groups of about 50 Seabees each would be needed to assemble the pontoon structure and have it ready for use in from three to four days. It was further estimated that 250 Seabees would be needed on board to operate the mobile floating airfield.

In further testing, the Floating Pontoon Flight Deck was towed to the open ocean in Rhode Island Sound, but it suffered damage. It was decided that using it in waters more turbulent than those of Narragansett Bay was not feasible. In addition, further field support would be needed, including fuel barges and living quarters for personnel. The experimental floating airfield was subsequently dismantled and the once promising Project Sock canceled. However, consideration of the concept has resurfaced many times since, most recently for use by the U.S. Navy in the smooth waters of the Persian Gulf.

10

A Connecticut WAVE
at Quonset Point

By Marie Virginia Murdock Duggins

Iwas the oldest of six children, born on February 27, 1919, in Pomfret, Connecticut (near the Rhode Island border), to a French Canadian mother and a first-generation American father of Scottish descent. During the earliest years of my life, we lived in Taftville, Connecticut, while my father apprenticed as a printer at a cotton mill. Later, my family moved to my grandparents' farm in rural Pomfret Landing, Connecticut, where my brothers, sisters and I grew up.

My father became a master printer at Cranston Print Works, commuting just over the border to Webster, Massachusetts. My mother had her hands full at home, raising my brothers, sisters and me and feeding and housing the two hired hands who worked the farm. I was happy and contented with my simple and innocent childhood. Following high school, I took a job at Pratt and Whitney in Willimantic, Connecticut, a company that manufactured airplane parts.

One evening late in 1943, four of my friends and I went to the movies. The theater showed a short movie about the war and the efforts of women in the service, mainly serving as nurses. None of us felt that we were doing anything very important, so we talked it over and decided to enlist. We all went to Norwich, Connecticut, to enlist together. When we got there, the Army Recruiters' Office was closed, but the Navy Recruiters' Office was still open so I enlisted in the U.S. Naval Reserve as a WAVE (which stood for Women Accepted for Volunteer Emergency Service).

I awaited my orders. I didn't go into the Navy right away. When I was inducted on January 13, 1944, I reported to Hunter College in New York City. Upon arriving at its Naval Training School in the Bronx, we weren't allowed to use the telephone for six weeks. Our training seemed mostly to learn to march in formation and do physical exercises to strengthen each of us.

Our training also corresponded with the jobs we'd be doing upon receiving our orders. Some of the WAVES were office workers because of their previous employment. As I was a certified machinist, my training concentrated on plane engines and the repairs I'd be making. There were all kinds of jobs, and we would be shipped to many different posts, depending on our assignments.

After our initial training, we were asked where we'd like to be stationed. I said, "California!" When asked why, I said that I'd always liked planes, from the first ride I'd taken on my father's farm to my work at Pratt and Whitney in Willimantic. I think that was why I was ultimately assigned to Naval Air Station Quonset Point, Rhode Island. Little by little, the thirty women with whom I'd trained were shipped out to different places, and we never saw one another again.

We finished our training and were excited to be leaving our training center and going to bases for deployment. We were so young and naive. When we got to Quonset Point, it was a disappointment. The hollering and cat-call whistles from the sailors at the mess hall were so loud—it was embarrassing!

We were so built up as to the importance of being a WAVE, I never looked back. Since my training had focused on plane part repair, I had a general idea of what I'd be doing. I was assigned to work in the A&R [Assembly & Repair (A&R) Unit] building as an Aviation Machinist Mate Third Class. The A&R building housed all the departments for repairing the aircrafts—engine parts, wiring, metal repair and so on.

Every so often, an aircraft carrier would come to Quonset with engines and parts from airplanes that had been downed in the ocean. All the parts needed to be cleaned of rust and repaired so that they could be returned and reused. My job was to clean the rust off the parts—gyros and engine parts.

In the hangar where I worked, there was a large vat with suspension chains hanging above it. It contained a chemical wash of acetone into which we'd submerge the rusted parts. The parts would soak for a time. When we removed them from the vat, we'd take them to our workstations to remove the rust. Sometimes it would take several washes before we could get them clean enough to send back. Although I never actually

Marie Duggins on graduation day after boot camp, 1944. *Duggins family.*

reassembled an engine, my next job was to learn where the part belonged in the plane's engine after the part passed inspection.

I felt my job, which I enjoyed, was an important job. We worked with several civilians; my boss was a civilian. At the time, I didn't think about liking or disliking my job because it was my assigned job, and I was helping the war effort. There was little discussion about anything outside our duties on base. I enjoyed being where I was and having the friends I'd made. Thoughts of war didn't worry me. I felt very safe and appreciated by my officers, all men.

There were no other women working where I worked. We chatted, and everyone was friendly. In fact, for my birthday one of the civilians made a tree out of wire to which dollar bills were attached. I don't remember how much money was on it, but I'll never forget how surprised I was!

There were two or three buildings that housed the WAVES on base. The buildings were filled with cubicles. Each cubicle housed four WAVES. There were two sets of bunk beds in each cubicle. There were shelves on which we placed our clothes. We were shown the correct way to fold our clothing—the way that the officers expected to see our clothes folded at inspections.

After settling into our quarters, we were placed in groups. We continued to do a lot of marching in formation, from our quarters to the chow hall, to our assigned jobs in the hangars or to offices and back again.

As the only women on base, we WAVES became friends. We quickly learned that we could get weekend leave from our officers if our cubicles were neat and clean. Every Friday, our captain would inspect our cubicles. A neat, clean cubicle meant a weekend pass to leave the base. If we had a long weekend, we'd go to the city, Providence. On the long weekends, we'd try to find someone who could drive us there.

We were always able to get a ride from a civilian. Of course, we had to wear our uniforms—navy blue in the winter, white in the summer. While there, we'd walk up and down the city streets and window shop. Occasionally, we'd get a drink before returning to Quonset. We had to have the right "snap-on" on our hats in order to get served a drink. We enjoyed ourselves, but we never did anything that would bring trouble to us or the navy station. We were never allowed to stay overnight, so we would catch a bus at several locations throughout the city for the trip back to Quonset.

Sometimes a few of us would go to the hangar. When a pilot had to go to pick up an entertainer who was coming to the base, we could get a ride to the destination. We couldn't get off the planes for these trips.

At other times, the pilots would fly to the Willimantic airport for bombing practice. If we went on those trips, we did have to get off. The pilot would tell us how long we could stay at the nearby bar, which was just over the hill. We'd still be in our coveralls and parachutes when we walked to the bar. We thought we were pretty big stuff when we'd walk into the establishment—the other patrons would stare at us. We never missed the flight back to base.

During our free time, many of us crocheted or knitted. It was also a time to write home or do any paperwork we had. Oftentimes some

Ruth A. Betts works on an airplane engine at Quonset Point's Assembly & Repair building. Marie Duggins and Ruth probably knew each other. *National Archives.*

of us would go for a walk together. Once in a while, the captain would offer us a steak dinner (officers were given a steak allowance) and have an outdoor platform for dancing, near the women's quarters. The steaks were delicious! A bunch of WAVES would start to dance, and soon the sailors would join us.

Also, we used to go to Crescent Park. Some of us would pick up clams. We'd simply open them and eat them raw. They were so good! Or we'd go swimming at Narragansett Pier. We were safe then—no worries about crime or rape. People were kinder back then.

The Naval Air Station at Quonset Point is where I met my husband, Fletcher "Bud" Duggins. Bud worked in an adjacent hangar to mine as a metalsmith. Everyone in that hangar worked on the plane engines that were brought for repair. He caught my eye while we were each marching in formation to or from the mess or our quarters. We were always in formation, in step, and singing from one place to another.

The rec hall was everyone's favorite spot on base. When not on duty, we could dance, play cards and relax. Bud and I simply started talking one day. I remember Bud came over to ask me to dance—he had his own style of dancing and loved to dance. No one else was on the dance floor. I told him that I didn't like to be the first one out on the dance floor. He asked if I'd mind if he danced with someone else. I said that I didn't, so he asked another WAVE to dance. The waltz began, and they won first place!

When he'd enter the mess hall for breakfast, he said he never had any problem finding me. He said he'd look for the tallest pile of toast, and there I'd be. He called me a Connecticut Yankee, and I called him a Rebel because he came from North Carolina.

If we didn't have a weekend leave, Bud and I would go to the rec hall—we'd sit and talk, dance, drink beer—Narragansett beer, of course.

One day, we were sitting on one of the benches in front of the mess hall, just talking. Bud was playing with a piece of wire. When I asked him what he was doing, he responded, "I'm making a ring for the girl I'm going to marry." I was so thrilled that I called my mother right away. I wore that ring for three days straight and had to take it off because it turned my finger green!

The first time I brought him home with me, I was worried about what he'd think. He'd talked about his life in Winston Salem. His mother was always working out in her garden, raising flowers that would be sent to New York City. At the time I'd enlisted, at our farm at Pomfret Landing, we had an outhouse on the hill behind the house, a pot under every bed, oil lamps and a hand-operated pump from which we'd get water. I didn't know what he'd think when he saw my home. But when we arrived home, to my surprise and pleasure, my father had electrified our home—and we had indoor plumbing!

My grandmother, who lived with us, liked Bud right away. Bud spoke no French, and she spoke no English. He was always a gentleman and could not abide swearing, especially in the presence of a woman.

We were married on November 24, 1944, while we were still in the navy. We got our papers in order and were married in the chapel on the base. Mickey and Joe Stoy, who were also stationed at Quonset, stood up for us. My mother, father and sister-in-law attended, along with my lieutenant. A reception followed at King's Wood, a lovely, big restaurant. My father paid for everything. When we returned to base, Bud went to his barracks, and I went to mine. Bud got quite a bit of kidding from the other sailors, as you can imagine.

I remember once Bud got me a blue ticket—a number 5. If I was caught off base without a pass, I could use the blue ticket to avoid punishment. I was proud of Bud for being able to get one for me.

Marines guarded the front gate, but no one guarded the back gate, as it was near the cemetery for planes that didn't fly anymore. A lot of us would jump the back gate and sneak out. Of course, if we'd been caught, we would have been in trouble. Except now I had a blue ticket.

One day there was a buzz circling through the base. It seemed like a long time before our captain made the announcement that the war was ended. On VJ Day everyone applauded and cheered—we were all so happy the war had ended. People were running to the telephones, and cars were driven through the base with sailors hooting and shouting that the war was over.

At news of the end of the war, I remember being happy because it meant I could go home. We were told we'd be stationed elsewhere so we should start packing in anticipation of shipping out, but Bud had to finish his tour at Quonset. I went to see my captain for permission to stay until Bud's tour ended in November 1945. I remained in the service so we could leave together. When our tours ended, somehow his discharge papers ended up in my barracks, and mine in his. As the captain read off each name and the women heard Bud's name instead of mine, they howled and hollered, "There's a man in the house!" Of course, no enlisted men were allowed in the women's quarters. Our service in the navy ended when we were honorably discharged at the U.S. Naval Barracks in Boston on November 9, 1945.

More Stories from Quonset Point and Davisville

By Christian McBurney

Union Influence in Military Contracting

Prior to America's entering World War II, unions were a powerful influence in Rhode Island. Here are a few anecdotes that reveal the continuing influence of unions during the war years.

In Providence, in the summer of 1940, seventeen-year-old Jack diPretoro sought a job helping to construct naval facilities at Quonset Point. For several days, he stood in line in North Kingstown without even speaking to the union representatives behind a counter accepting job applications and doing the hiring. Meanwhile, others jumped the line. The frustrated teenager mentioned his difficulties to his father, who, the next day, traveled by train to Quonset with his son and barged ahead of the line to speak with the union hiring representatives. Somehow diPretoro was hired that day. He helped build ammunition bunkers on Hope Island. Once, he saw a sign at the station asking for civilian volunteers to work at the navy base at Pearl Harbor. He later wondered if any workers accepted the offer and, if they did, whether they survived December 7. (DiPretoro became an experienced combat fighter pilot in the Pacific, and in April 1945 he returned to fly TBF/TBM Avenger aircraft in Narragansett Bay, with his crew practicing torpedo launches.)

During the war, another seventeen-year-old, Marion Cheever of East Greenwich, served as a backup courier at Davisville, carrying correspondence from the George A. Fuller Company to navy officers, "a distance of five barracks," she remembered. Her father was a senior executive with the George A. Fuller Company, the main builder of the navy facilities at Davisville and Quonset Point. She recalled that when the transport ships at the Advance Base Depot needed to be loaded, buses arrived from Fox Point in Providence carrying stevedores (longshoremen). The longshoremen's union demanded cash payments. With stevedores in short supply, navy officials obliged. Marion was directed to get the cash to pay the stevedores from a local bank called Union Trust. She was assigned a marine carrying a submachine gun. When they arrived at the bank, the marine ordered that no one leave and/or enter. The young marine, with his submachinegun at the ready, guarded the door. The marine then escorted Cheever, with cash in hand, back to the barracks. The cash was stuffed into envelopes, ready to be handed out to stevedores as they boarded buses back to Fox Point.

J. Allen Bell, an officer who stayed at NAS Quonset Point for the month of July 1944, had some choice words about civilian (including union) workers in the busy Assembly & Repair Unit that performed important work repairing aircraft engines, including those for his unit's PV-1 Ventura seaplanes. In a letter to his wife, Bell complained that the civilian workers at A&R "stand around all day and talk and argue politics. The Navy hasn't a thing to say about running this place and the civilians brag about it." Bell said he was told that civilian workers "can put a sailor on report, get him transferred or restricted. They can do the same for officers too." Bell was informed that the wife of Rhode Island's powerful U.S. senator Theodore F. Green, a strong union supporter, owned a share of the bus company servicing the station. "Senator Green runs this station and everything connected with it and they all admit it," Bell raged to his wife. He added menacingly, "I'm sure glad I'm not stationed to this place because the lid is going to blow off someday and the axe is going to fall." No doubt the claims of civilian control were exaggerated, but there could have been an inkling of truth that navy brass had to pay heed to the civilian workers, as they were performing crucial tasks repairing planes, many of which traveled on aircraft carriers to Pacific war zones. Bell may have been a bit of a crank. The Assembly & Repair Unit proved to be very effective in repairing and maintaining aircraft. Bell's experience contrasts with Marie Duggins's positive interaction with her civilian coworkers, as indicated in the prior chapter.

Merchant ships at a pier at the Advance Base Depot at Davisville on September 11, 1943, wait to be loaded with cargo by stevedores before heading to distant U.S. Navy bases around the world. *National Archives.*

Most Rhode Island defense workers worked long and hard hours, feeling it was their duty to support the soldiers and sailors at the front. For example, Herreshoff Shipyard at Bristol built one hundred small vessels for the navy. Herreshoff Manufacturing Company's president, T.F. Haffenreffer, proclaimed in late 1945, "No shipyard, large or small, here or abroad, can point to a finer record of uninterrupted production—production unhampered by petty grievances or disputes—an outstanding accomplishment in harmonious teamwork by Herreshoff craftsmen and management…and a real contribution to winning the War."

RICHARD NIXON TRAINS AT QUONSET POINT (AUGUST–OCTOBER 1942)

Quonset Point had a naval aviation "indoctrination" school, called the Naval Training School, for newly minted navy officers, many fresh from college with no naval background. The school provided a basic knowledge of naval customs, usage, nomenclature, military law, hygiene and drill. The short program's most famous graduate was twenty-nine-year-old Richard Nixon, who, following his appointment as lieutenant junior grade in the U.S. Naval Reserve, began indoctrination training in August 1942. Nixon had been a lawyer for the Office of Emergency Management and was living with his wife, Pat, in Washington, D.C., when he volunteered. Later, as president, Nixon appointed William Rogers as secretary of state. Nixon once joked with Rogers, "We met 32 years ago at Quonset Point when we were both one of the lowest forms of life, I mean lieutenants, junior grade, in the United States Navy Reserve." One of their classmates called their training "very demanding, physically and mentally." Nixon completed the training in October 1942.

First assigned to help build an air base at Ottumwa, Iowa, Nixon volunteered for sea duty. He was assigned as officer in charge of the South Pacific Air Transport Command (SCAT) at Guadalcanal and later served at Bougainville and Green Island. His unit prepared manifests and flight plans for C-47 operations and supervised the loading and unloading of cargo aircraft. For this work, Nixon was awarded a Letter of Commendation. He was promoted to lieutenant on October 1, 1943. In January 1944, at Bougainville, his small SCAT command was bombed by the Japanese

Lieutenant (j.g.) Richard Nixon, Naval Reserve, stands second from the far left in the top row in his class photograph at the Naval Training School at Quonset Point. *Christian McBurney Collection.*

twenty-eight nights out of thirty. His role lacked glory but was important, and he was liked by the personnel under his command.

Ironically, it was under the Nixon administration that NAS Quonset Point suffered substantial budget cuts and closure. It was officially decommissioned on June 28, 1974.

JOSEPH PURDY WRITES OF THE NAVAL INDOCTRINATION SCHOOL AT QUONSET POINT

Set forth here are excerpts from letters of 26-year-old Lieutenant Joseph Purdy, who attended the Naval Training School (informally known as indoctrination school) at Quonset Point from June to August 1942, just before Richard Nixon attended. Purdy, hailing from Pikesville, Maryland, prior to the war was a junior executive with the Baltimore Gas & Electric Company. All of his letters were sent to his wife, Genevieve, at a time when they had two young children. In the letters, time is expressed in military terms. (For example, 1500 hours is 3:00 p.m.).

Purdy graduated high enough in his class so that after completing indoctrination school, he was selected for the Air Combat Intelligence School at Quonset, attending from August to October 1942. Purdy then served in the Pacific on the aircraft carrier USS *Intrepid* (now a museum moored in the Hudson River in New York City), when Japanese kamikaze aircraft crashed into it off Luzon in the Philippines on November 25, 1944. After serving on USS *Siboney*, he was promoted to lieutenant commander. He survived the war and returned to Maryland. Purdy is an example of the many graduates of Quonset's Air Combat Intelligence School who, before the war, had been experienced business executives or lawyers and who, after departing Quonset, provided important services to commanders of aircraft carriers and admirals commanding carrier task forces in the Pacific theater.

June 18:

> *Arrived here* [Naval Air Station Quonset Point] *on June 17 at approximately 0900. The first order was to remove all insignia and change to khaki—the only uniform we* [Purdy and other officer classmates] *will wear while on the post. Then we signed in, were issued our bed linen and told to make up our bunks. Mine is #381 in Compartment 7A and is the upper bunk.*

June 22:

Our days are so crowded that it is almost impossible to summarize them. However, I will try to give you an idea of what we are doing:

0600	*Reveille*
0715	*Breakfast*
0805	*Muster and marching to class*
0830	*Divine Service*
0840–0930	*Fundamentals of Naval Service* [class]
0940–1030	*Navy Regulations* [class]
1040–1130	*Courts and Boards* [class]
1200–1300	*Dinner*
1315	*Inspection*
1330	*Muster and marching to class*
1340–1430	*Introduction to Naval Aviation* [class]
1430–1545	*Drill*
1545–1630	*Athletics*
1730–1815	*Supper*
1900–2100	*Study period*
2200	*Taps*

In addition there is also a class on seamanship that meets 3 times a week; we have a weekly quiz in each subject; a weekly seminar in each subject and we must rearrange our notes in final form. We have also been issued 17 books for required, collateral reading. We make our own beds and care for our own quarters. We have liberty from 1500 on Saturday to 0630 on Monday. As long as we are "aboard ship" (i.e., at the Station) we must attend church on Sundays. (I forgot to mention that before long we must start a course on World War II!).

All terms used at the Station are the same as those used aboard ship—bed bunk, floor-deck, wall, bulkhead, fore, aft port, starboard, etc.

June 29:

I never worked so hard and so long in my life. Every working day is 17 hours long (and I mean actual work) except Saturday which is only nine hours: Sunday is our only free day and then if we are aboard [at the Station], we must go to church. The Navy places a lot of emphasis on

Officers graduating from the Naval Training School at Quonset Point stand at attention at their graduation ceremony in an auditorium, June 12, 1942. *National Archives.*

church attendance and it is a court-martial offense to be irreverent in church. All commanding officers are charged with the duty of holding church except under battle conditions. I have enjoyed it thoroughly just as I have enjoyed everything else here.

We really are learning a lot and I believe we will be good Naval airmen when we come out. We have the C.O.'s [commanding officer's] permission to cut classes anytime we can arrange to get off the ground. (That is, to fly). We are still drilling about two hours a day and my feet (and many hundreds of others) are still sore. Our platoon is about the worst in the outfit when it comes to marching. However, if you come up to graduation, I think you will be proud of all of us.

July 14:

Since I talked with you last we have had pistol practice and I got one bull's eye out of twenty shots; the 19 other Germans or Japs will be just as safe as if they were at home. And maybe the one, in actual combat, will forget to stand still—then they will all be safe. We are drilling with rifles now (Springfield's, vintage of '98) and after an hour or so they make one's shoulder sore. However I can go through the Manual of Arms like a veteran.

July 21:

Last Saturday we were invited to the Dunes Club, a very exclusive beach club similar to Gibson Island. There was a dinner dance in the evening followed by a bathing party Sunday afternoon. George Race, Charley Woollen and I stayed at a summer hotel, the Breakers, Saturday night, for $2.75 each. We had separate rooms and a marvelous breakfast Sunday morning. We went swimming in the ocean Sunday afternoon and then came back to the base to the Officers Club for dinner.

July 30:

[T]his afternoon our billets were read out and I was among those selected for Air Combat Intelligence School. This is supposed to be the top billet of them all and, as you know, is exactly what I had been hoping for. We will

Two escort carriers at a pier at Quonset Point, waiting for their repaired fighter aircraft to be loaded onto their decks, June 22, 1945. These "baby carriers," effective at hunting German submarines, frequently visited Narragansett Bay and were also used in the Pacific theater. Air combat intelligence officers such as Joseph Purdy often served on carriers. *Naval History and Heritage Command.*

have leave from Friday August 14 to Saturday August 22 and then return to enter the Intelligence School at Quonset. On or about Oct. 22, we will graduate (if everything goes well), and then we may be sent "anywhere in the world." Unquestionably it will be somewhere outside the United States. We will be officers while we are in the school (instead of weekend officers as we are now) and will get a chance to do a great deal of flying.

Purdy wrote letters to his wife during the time he attended Air Combat Intelligence School too, but he included no information about his courses, as it was confidential.

Female Parachute Packers at Quonset Point Save Pilot Lives

During the war, packing parachutes was performed largely by women, including at the A&R parachute shop at NAS Quonset Point. Harold R. Brown, head of the "chute shop," believed that women were both better at using special tools to pleat and pack the huge silk parachutes and "more apt to spot something wrong." Of course, disaster could occur if a pilot jumped out of his airplane and his parachute failed to open or its lines got tangled up when the silk canopy unfolded. Pilots, recognizing the importance of packers, sometimes sent them gifts. In the summer of 1943, the *Quonset Scout* newspaper reported that a navy pilot sent a box of chocolates to senior packer Marge Jenner of Wickford for "saving his skin when he was forced to bail out in a parachute folded and packed on the long tables at the A&R shop at Quonset." The pilot found Jenner's card in his parachute, indicating she had packed his parachute. Jenner, originally from Augusta, Maine, was the first woman to make a parachute jump in New England. The shop's other certified senior packers included Mary DiBona of Providence, Steffie Tessitore and Mildred Carium.

The *Quonset Scout* reported in April 1944 that Rose Quinlan of Warwick, a "parachute packing grandma of the A&R parachute shop," learned that her son, "piloting a Navy fighter plane in the South Pacific, had got his first Jap bomber. In addition, the parachute shop soon expects that Mrs. Quinn will be rated as a licensed parachute mechanic by the Civil Aeronautics Authority after months of apprenticeship at the delicate art of 'chute packing.'"

The tragic consequence of a parachute failing to open occurred in Rhode Island, on July 21, 1943, when Lieutenant Charles Newton Lovely, a twenty-one-year-old Londoner with the Royal Navy training at Quonset Point, was on a routine flight. His Corsair caught fire and he was forced to bail out over the Sakonnet River near the Stone Bridge, but his parachute failed to open and he fell to his death.

Aviation Gunnery School at Quonset Point

The latest technology was used to train pilots at Quonset Point. For example, "Link Trainers" in concrete silos were used to teach pilots how to rely on celestial navigation to fly their planes when they were over the ocean or otherwise far away from friendly radio signals. As another example, a low-pressure chamber familiarized flight crews with the effects of flying at high altitudes. Simpler technology was used too, such as movie projectors.

Hector Asselin of Warren, Rhode Island, enlisted in the navy at age twenty. In his application, when asked about his hobbies, he jotted down working with movie projectors. He was ordered to NAS Quonset Point—to perform maintenance work. Months later, he and thirteen others on his work crew were sent to Detroit, Michigan, to learn how to train pilots using movie projectors. Pilots would be taught to identify Japanese and German warships by viewing their silhouettes projected onto a screen. Rear gunners on navy fighter planes were also brought in for refresher training. One projector would show an enemy plane approaching, and another would show where

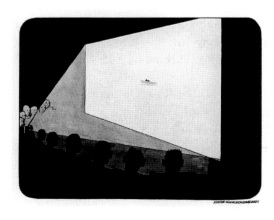

Cartoon poking fun at training for Quonset Point pilots to identify warships from above. The caption to this cartoon says: "In a tenth of a second, anyone should be able to see that it's not the *Tennessee*—notice the aft stack (?). It's shorter than the bridge, so that makes it impossible to confuse it with the *South Dakota*—also it would be 2A1. You should be able to get those twin over triple turrets in a flash—that being a dead give-away for the *Nevada*. Next slide." *Christian McBurney Collection.*

the rear gunner was supposed to fire—in an arc ahead of it. Asselin was assigned to the Aviation Free Gunnery Unit at Quonset Point, which opened December 1942. It offered a five-week course in air gunnery.

In a 2002 interview, Asselin recalled a large aircraft carrier arriving at Quonset Point. It was probably USS *Ranger*, the only large carrier that visited Quonset Point during the war. In January 1944, it returned to Quonset from active service in the invasion of North Africa and in the North Sea off Germany. "There was some word that they (gunners on fighter aircraft) were having problems knocking those planes down that were attacking them," said the Rhode Island native. He remembered one of the gunners "wasn't doing well at all, and I had to reject him….[H]e got mad with me." Asselin continued, "Coming into town, I kept thinking, 'Boy, I'd better keep looking around over my shoulder,' but I had him come back and he did alright later on with a few more refresher [courses]." Overall, Asselin was impressed by the accuracy of the gunners: "Most of them were right on the tee."

Harbor Entrance Command Post at Fort Burnside in Jamestown

By Varoujan Karentz

With all the important navy bases and facilities, as well as shipbuilding and other defense contractors, surrounding Narragansett Bay during World War II, the need to protect them became a paramount concern. On October 2, 1941, Secretary of War Henry Stimson directed that a Harbor Entrance Command Post (HECP) be established for the protection of seventeen strategic harbors in the continental United States. One of them was planned for Narragansett Bay. According to army coastal defense doctrine, a HECP's function was "to collect and disseminate information of activities in the defensive sea area, to control unescorted commercial shipping in the defensive coastal area, and to take prompt and decisive action to operate the elements of the harbor and coastal defenses, in order to deny enemy action within the defensive coastal area."

Beavertail Point on Conanicut Island, with views over Narragansett Bay's two main entrances, provided the ideal location for a HECP. It was one of only two sites designated for the highest level of mission complexity. In addition to the control of shipping and harbor surveillance, the HECP at Beavertail was also tasked with preventing enemy ships from penetrating defenses, laying mines or scuttling themselves to block the harbor entrance and warding off German motor torpedo boats.

On December 4, 1941, three days before the Japanese attack on Pearl Harbor, the southern portion of Beavertail was officially named Fort Burnside. Established through the acquisition of 185.22 acres of land by both condemnation and purchase, mostly in mid-1942, Fort Burnside was located exactly within the present boundaries of Beavertail State Park.

Detailed procedures were established to ensure proper recognition of military warships and merchant ships and to determine whether they were allowed to enter Narragansett Bay. Any unexpected arrivals, unusual features of ship superstructure, crew appearance, delayed arrival or incorrect signals created concern about enemy deception. When an unidentified vessel entered the defensive area, the HECP would direct a visual challenge by flashing a signal light or signal flags. If an immediate response to the proper code was not received, the HECP implemented counter measures. At night, the area was to be illuminated with searchlights. Gun batteries based at Fort Burnside and other forts covering the East and West Passages were trained immediately on a suspect vessel, and the vessel would be ordered to stop until an examining officer boarded the vessel and notified the HECP.

If the intruder failed to stop, a warning shot could be fired from a coastal gun battery and a patrol vessel could be dispatched to investigate. The submarine net gates would remain closed, and minefields could be activated from the "safe" position. The gun batteries could sink the ship, if appropriate.

All communications to various defense command locations from and to the HECP were conducted by a network of landline telephones, backed up by two-way radio equipment. Flashing light and flag signals were used to communicate with ships as necessary at observation posts located at nearby Forts Getty, Wetherill, Varnum, Greene and Adams.

Prospect Hill, the highest point on Beavertail, was the original location of the primary observation posts for various gun batteries and mine commands on Conanicut Island, as well as secondary observation posts for other nearby coastal batteries. In late 1941 or early 1942, a joint army-navy defense team first constructed a wooden twelve-by-thirty-foot observation shack located south of the present Beavertail Lighthouse beyond the road on the rock ledge and about 75 feet west of the base of the original Beavertail Lighthouse. Subsequently, a second observation post was built north of the lighthouse to command the entrance to the West Passage.

Fort Burnside fell under the command of an army officer, even though the HECP was a joint operation with the navy technically in command. Fully functional in 1943, nine officers and forty enlisted men at the HECP operated its underwater and surface surveillance tracking systems, supplemented with radios, visual signaling devices and telephones. War Department directives required that the HECP have both an army and a navy officer on watch during all shifts. The operating crews were billeted at nearby Fort Getty.

Aerial image of Fort Burnside at Beavertail Point on Jamestown in 1946, showing the Coast Guard Station at the southern tip, the Harbor Entrance Command Post in the middle on a rise of land and radar antennae behind it on the left. In the distance on the left is Spraycliff Observatory. *Jamestown Historical Society.*

Battery 213, named "Whiting," with two 3-inch guns, was relocated from Fort Getty to Fort Burnside during the summer of 1942, after construction of new magazine and gun platforms was completed. The battery was on the eastern perimeter of the enclave facing Brenton Point across the East Passage. In 1943, two 6-inch steel-shielded guns on barbette carriages were installed overlooking the West Passage.

In addition to Battery Whiting being ready to fire at any suspicious vessels that failed to cooperate with the HECP, it had a secondary mission as an anti-motor torpedo boat battery (AMTB). The HECP was concerned about the risk of German freighters, called Q boats, launching motor torpedo boats that could penetrate net defenses and fire torpedoes at targets in Narragansett Bay.

At the very southeast end of the peninsula on the grounds of Beavertail Lighthouse, dug in and heavily sandbagged, was a rapid-fire AMTB cannon. Three 90-millimeter gun batteries located at Fort Varnum on the mainland in Narragansett overlooking the West Passage, and Forts Getty and Wetherill on Jamestown also provided anti–motor torpedo boat protection. Mobile 3-inch guns could be used too.

The command/observation posts on Prospect Hill and the shack in front of Beavertail Lighthouse remained in operation until July 1, 1943, when a substantial building was constructed by the U.S. Army Engineers to serve as the HECP headquarters building. It was formally identified as "Bombproof Cottage C-1." It was the most expensive HECP constructed in the nation during the war, and it still stands today (see chapter 18).

The two-story 24-room HECP building that supported the gun batteries was constructed of reinforced concrete, in some sections as much as 3-feet thick. Its footprint measures 69 feet across the base by 53 feet, 6 inches. Disguised as a large farm residence, it even had livestock grazing nearby.

This is a current view of the Harbor Entrance Command Post. Even though it is now rented as a private residence, radar and radio towers installed by the navy after the war still stand at the site. *Norman Desmarais.*

The exterior is decorated with stucco, wood trim, false porches, wood railings and cedar shingles. On the north side, three false windows with wood trim are painted on the concrete wall of the radio room. A series of rectangular viewing ports with protective shutters lined both the first and second floors.

A deckhouse on top of the second floor housed a signal station where personnel could use old methods of communication when more modern technology failed. Personnel could operate selectable colored lights and raise color-coded signal flags to acknowledge signals to and from naval and merchant shipping. Fort Varnum in Narragansett, with a view of western Beavertail Point, still has a fire-control post standing with a room used as an observation post that includes brightly colored stencil drawings of flags that guided soldiers using flags to communicate with offshore ships. (See this book's back cover for color photographs.)

HECP personnel in second-floor rooms served as observers and spotters for Battery Whiting and other nearby batteries. They were located in four rooms, called visual sighting stations, manned by observers with optical azimuth and range-finding instruments. Telescopes and binoculars were standard equipment used for surveillance and to read signals from vessels. Later, radar bearing and range information supplemented the visual observers, especially during periods of poor visibility. Thick concrete walls separated the four rooms, in case one was hit by enemy fire.

Sections of the first floor were wooden partitions built for camouflage purposes only. They contained no tactical equipment other than the first-floor radio room, which was surrounded by concrete blast walls.

The basement contained the target plotting room and operations center where the seaward defense commander or operations duty officer and his staff were located. A large, colored wall map of the defended area was painted on a sheet of steel, showing the coastline from Montauk on Long Island to Block Island, to Cuttyhunk in the Elizabeth Islands of Buzzards Bay and beyond. It was marked with a grid also showing the range arcs of the coastal gun batteries. All targets reported by observers or radar were positioned on the map with magnets and were manually moved to track the vessel. The harbor defenses of New Bedford provided information about all ships headed southwest from the Cape Cod Canal, while harbor defenses of Long Island Sound reported eastbound traffic.

Radar area coverage charts showed the overlapping fields of other radars located on Block Island and Long Island Sound and along Buzzards Bay. Land obstructions that interrupted radar coverage were noted on the map.

The HECP building burst with special systems and technologically advanced equipment for the era. Special vents and steel blast doors were installed, including a concrete escape hatch from the basement. An air filtration system protected the occupants from gas attacks. Valves vented any poison gas while clean air was sucked in and filtered. Dehumidifiers and air conditioning (relatively new concepts) were installed in the basement. The floors were covered with linoleum tiles and the ceilings were covered with acoustical tile.

The 243rd Coast Artillery Regimental Commander, the assigned intelligence officer and the operations duty officer had desks with telephones in front of the plotting board. A navy officer, representing Naval Operating Base Newport, reported underwater intelligence information from the basement cable room. This surveillance room was off-limits to army personnel. Access was never granted to any area within the HECP to anyone not assigned there. Nonessential conversations with others, even between army and navy personnel, were also discouraged.

The army officers and soldiers assigned to the HECP were a combination of Rhode Island National Guard and regular army. Each gun battery provided one man as an observer for each shift, thus permitting the observer to communicate with his own unit. Their supervisor hailed from the Fort Adams Battalion Headquarters in Newport.

As the war progressed, younger officers were sent overseas and replaced by older men shipped in from distant posts. Soldiers with minor disabilities rendering them unfit for combat were assigned as observer replacements for men who were physically more fit for combat. Beginning in 1944, as the enemy naval threat diminished and the American armed forces went on the offensive in Europe, substantial numbers of soldiers from Narragansett Bay defenses were assigned to field artillery units destined for overseas roles. Although these personnel reductions affected gun battery efficiency, the HECP still effectively controlled traffic in and out of Narragansett Bay. At the same time, upgraded radar, aircraft and blimp capabilities supplemented early warning efforts.

Personnel stationed at the HECP at Fort Burnside had at their disposal an impressive array of the most recent technological equipment that could be deployed to identify potential enemy ships and submarines.

To help thwart potential penetration of the Narragansett Bay defenses by German submarines or motor torpedo boats, the HECP was provided with illumination capabilities. Searchlights had been used to help defend Narragansett Bay since the early 1900s, but these were larger than ever. Battery I (Searchlight Battery) of the 243rd Coast Artillery deployed carbon-arc searchlights, each sixty inches in diameter and enclosed in aluminum, on two towers on the base of the previous observation shack in front of the Beavertail Lighthouse. Electric motors positioned the azimuth and elevation of the light controlled from HECP.

Late in the war, the 60-inch lights were replaced by similar searchlights mounted on portable wheeled vehicles near the West Passage. Residents reported numerous occasions during the war when searchlight beams illuminated the sky. Beginning in January 1941, trailer-mounted acoustical listening horns supplemented the searchlights as an aid to detecting the bearing of aircraft sounds.

The second deck of the HECP included 12-inch incandescent lamp blinker signal-type searchlights. This signaling device used Morse Code. Since this approach was more secure than radio contact, it was the preferred method to communicate with ships arriving at Narragansett Bay.

The navy employed a unique underwater electronic loop detection system. It consisted of two loops of submarine magnetic detection cable 90,185 feet long laid on the floor of the bay just south of Beavertail Point. It extended across the entrances of the East and West Passages. The cables originated at the HECP and were long enough to return across the bay and terminate at the HECP. The cables were laid in precise patterns on the seabed. The loops were oriented east to west, opposite to the earth's terrestrial magnetic field variation, permitting sensitive calibration. When a steel-hulled vessel (ship or submarine) crossed over the loops and distorted the calibrated field, sensitive galvanometers and flux meters registered minute levels of electrical distortion in the cables, causing needles in the HECP monitored by navy sonar specialists to swing. The signals were detected, amplified and transmitted to listening equipment in the HECP. Direction and speed could be calculated when a vessel crossed two points of the loop array. The navy removed the detection loops on July 16, 1944, even though the war with Germany was still ongoing. The removal suggested either that the loops were not particularly accurate or that the German threat to Narragansett Bay had receded and resources were needed elsewhere.

According to a 1943 Coastal Defense sketch, two underwater hydrophone systems in the East and West Passages enabled audible detection, as well as limited classification and identification of propulsion engines. Experienced sonar operators could identify specific vessels by their own unique acoustical characteristics. Hydrophones collecting audible signatures were not effective against quiet submarines or those that could attempt to turn off their engines and drift into the harbor with the tide. The underwater hydrophone coupling cables were routed from the HECP to the Mine Casement Control and then went to the cable huts at Hull's Cove and Austin Hollow.

Two new radar systems were installed at the HECP in early June 1944. The new SCR 582 radar system could detect ships (including fast-moving torpedo boats) and communicate the exact range and azimuth to the ship. It was also capable of detecting low-flying aircraft. The radar system was primarily used at night and in low visibility conditions. It was developed by the RadLab team from the Massachusetts Institute of Technology (MIT) and built by Western Electric Company. It had a ten-centimeter wavelength with a peak power of fifty thousand watts. The conical narrow beam radar antenna was located on top of the HECP building.

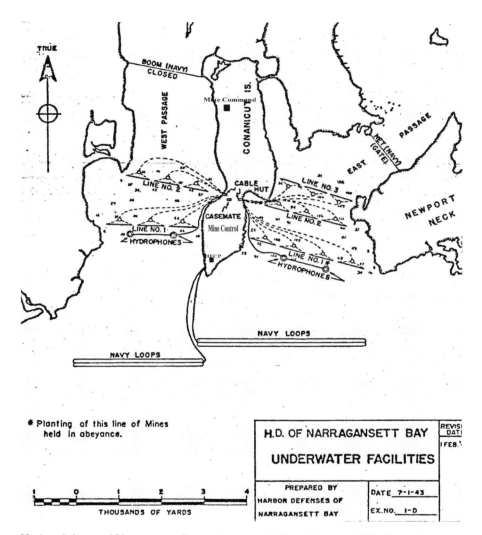

Harbor defenses of Narragansett Bay, underwater facilities, February 1945. Revised by Varoujan Karentz to show HECP and Mine Command. *National Archives.*

The targets were displayed on a 360-degree cathode ray tube at the HECP. In ideal conditions, the radar's effective range was 90,000 yards, but at Fort Burnside the range was reduced due to the low hill on which the 42-inch parabolic reflector was installed and the impact of the curvature of the earth. A triangular wire mesh reflector screen installed on Block Island aided radar range and sensitivity calibration.

The SCR 296-A radar permitted the operation of army guns and searchlights at their maximum range, instead of a visual range determined by whether it was daytime or good weather. Also designed by MIT and manufactured by Western Electric Company, it was installed on a 100-foot skeleton tower about 200 yards north of the HECP. The radar tower was shrouded with a conical top and painted to look like a water tower from a distance.

Once a vessel or submarine was detected visually or by the SCR 582 radar, the SCR 296-A was trained on the target to determine the range and azimuth. The data would be telephoned to the battery plotting room. This radar did not sweep in a 360-degree arc like the SCR 582 but showed only a narrow sector controlled by the radar operator. The radar set, consisting of many different electronic components contained in a large cabinet and arranged on a large table, required a crew of four men to operate: a range operator, a range reader, an azimuth operator and an azimuth reader. The transmitter was located in the base of the tower.

The United States Army Signal Corps operated the SCR 582 and SCR 296-A radar systems. To keep them alert, operators were supposed to be changed every thirty minutes. (SCR 296-A radar systems were also located in Rhode Island at Block Island (east side), Green Hill Beach, Fort Greene, Brenton Point, Sachuest Point and Warren Point.)

To facilitate command and control, the HECP and other coast defense posts along Narragansett Bay were hooked together by a "hot loop" telephone line to the 36th Anti-Aircraft Brigade and the Regional Defense Command in Boston. Fort Adams Newport Harbor Defense first screened all reports. The telephone system, installed by Western Electric Company, included 100 separate lines terminating in the HECP. There were direct line communications among Naval Operating Base Newport, Fort Adams and the HECP. Telephone lines from HECP were connected to local coastal gun batteries for firing coordination and to casemates located on Prospect Hill and at Hull Cove, where mine command and fire-control centers were located.

Because they could be intercepted by the enemy, radio communications were to be used in emergencies only when the telephone system failed. A complete radio network connected the HECP, Fort Adams in Newport, Fort Varnum in Narragansett, the Prospect Hill casemate and the boats of the mine and net tending fleet. The equipment at all stations included SCR-281 (1.8–2.7 MHz AM voice) radio transmitters and receivers. However, mine yawls (small mine-tending vessels) were equipped only with hand-held 1-watt BC 611–type single-channel walkie-talkie transceivers.

Antisubmarine nets and antitorpedo boat booms were employed in both the East Passage and West Passage to prevent enemy vessels from entering Narragansett Bay. The first net, laid in 1941 before the outbreak of war late that year, was located across the East Passage between Fort Wetherill on Conanicut Island and the west shore south of Fort Adams at Newport Neck. The second net was laid a year later from Fort Getty on Conanicut Island across the West Passage to Fort Kearney in Narragansett (currently occupied by the University of Rhode Island's Narragansett Bay Campus).

The first nets consisted of segments of heavy chain hung from buoys. Early in the war, the chain nets were replaced by cable-type fifteen-inch ring nets. Gates in the net to allow ship traffic were installed only in the East Passage. Net minders onboard patrol boats out of Fort Wetherill manned the gates as directed by the HECP. Net-tending vessels, including the USS *Yazoo* and USS *Tonawanda*, would show different visual day or lighted night

A double layer of antisubmarine nets in the East (Main) Channel extends from Fort Wetherill on Jamestown to south of Fort Adams, May 28, 1942. Two small Net Gate Vessels and one Net Tender monitor the nets, allowing boat traffic in and out, while two artillery pieces can be seen at Fort Wetherill. In the lower right are barracks and administrative buildings. *National Archives.*

signals for incoming or outgoing traffic, alerting ship commanders whether the gates were open or closed.

In 1942, the West Passage and the Sakonnet River were closed to all maritime traffic except specially licensed traffic such as military craft and local fishing boats. Because the Sakonnet River was so shallow, it was not deemed necessary to place nets across it.

A floating boom device was used in conjunction with the nets in the West Passage. One configuration consisted of large floating wooden blocks or timbers anchored to the bottom, shackled together with two parallel steel cables that had enormous protruding barbs. It was expected that an enemy boat seeking to get past the boom would avoid ramming the floating blocks and instead run over the cable barbs, which would rip open the bottom of the boat. (Some locals recalled that while the West Passage nets had no gates, tending vessels would swing open the boom to allow authorized fishing vessels access to and from the sea. Others claimed that local fishing boats with shallow drafts simply rode over the West Passage's barbed cables, which were below the surface.)

Melville, in Portsmouth, hosted the Naval Net Depot and training command for Coastal Net Detachments in New England. The Net Training School, one of two established in 1941, closed in 1944.

Another defensive system consisted of submerged mines packed with dynamite planted to the north of the antisubmarine nets. Mines were primarily intended to prevent enemy submarines from slipping up Narragansett Bay, but they could also deter enemy surface vessels.

In the early part of the war, buoyant mines with explosive charges of 100 to 500 pounds of TNT were planted in Narragansett Bay. Attached by cables to anchors, they floated about fifteen feet below the surface. These mines could be set for "contact fire," "delayed contact fire" or "observation fire." Contact fire mines would explode when a ship came into physical contact with it. Observation fire first required the target vessel either to contact the mine, which would alert personnel in the casemate or be seen from an observation station. HECP personnel then had to determine if the ship was enemy or friendly. If enemy, upon direction from the HECP, personnel manning the mine control casemate at Hull Cove could fire a mine electronically. But because the buoyant mines were only fifteen feet below the water's surface, passing ships sometimes fouled the connecting cables.

M4 ground mines replaced some of the buoyant mines in the East and West Passages. Ground mines were attached by cable to the bay's floor. In

February 1942, six groups of mines, with each group having 19 buoyant mines or 13 ground mines, were planted in two lines in the East and West Passages. A postwar ordnance disposal report stated that 234 M4 mines were recovered, in addition to 291 other types of mines.

In 1943, a new generation of mines replaced the older contact-type mines. These ground mines lay on the seabed, filled with upward of three thousand pounds of TNT. They were cone-shaped to minimize the risk of enemy minesweeping vessels displacing them. These new mines would send a signal to the control station if a ship of over one thousand tons passed over. The control station could then electronically fire the mines when given the authority or place a specific field in an automatic mode to detonate when its sensing mechanism detected a target. The ground mines could also be cleared without danger by friendly ships.

All mines were connected by electrical cables to MC1 and MC2 huts located at Hull Cove and Austin Hollow in Jamestown. These structures, although deteriorating, still stand. From there underground extension cables went into the mine control casemate located three-quarters of a mile north of the HECP off the west side of Beavertail Road. The Hull Cove Mine Casemate was a reinforced concrete underground structure containing rooms with banks of lights and activation switches from where the location of the mines and their targets could be plotted and the mines fired.

The mine casemate at Hull Cove was under the direction of HECP and the Mine Command Post on Prospect Hill. Personnel manning the Mine Command Post on Prospect Hill would inform HECP when a ship or submarine contacted a mine. The seaward defense commander or operations duty officer could then order mine command to fire one or more mines to destroy the intruder. It was understood that firing too many mines would open a corridor, allowing an intruder to enter the harbor after a decoy attack.

The 10th Coast Artillery Regiment, headquartered at Fort Adams, had units at Fort Wetherill and at Fort Varnum. These units and their flotilla of mine vessels planted and controlled the minefields. East Passage mines were controlled from Fort Wetherill until the Hull Cove Mine Casemate was completed. Another mine complex at Fort Getty serviced the West Passage.

The navy expressed concern about possible accidental damage or sinking of navy vessels from the detonation of a friendly mine. To the dismay of the army mine commander, orders required the HECP to place the entire mine system on safe status when any navy ship entered or left Narragansett Bay.

The value of the extensive defenses controlled by the HECP, and their ability to deter enemy ships and submarines from entering Narragansett

This fascinating and rare photograph shows U.S. Army soldiers marching with a surprising variety of uniforms and headgear into Fort Varnum in March 1944. Soldiers stationed on Jamestown and at other forts on the coast in Rhode Island may have had a similar look. *Rhode Island Army National Guard.*

Bay, may never be fully understood. In 1944, the navy claimed that the value of underwater surveillance nationwide "is evident from the fact that not one effective penetration into any harbor anywhere, guarded by US harbor detection equipment has been made since the midget Japanese submarine slipped into Pearl Harbor on December 7th 1941." During the entire war period, all coastal military facilities in Rhode Island remained unmolested by the enemy.

The only military incidents that occurred within viewing distance of the HECP was the German U-boat *853*'s sinking of the SS *Black Point* on May 5, 1945, and the sinking of the U-boat by U.S. Navy and Coast Guard destroyer escorts later the same day. (Both sinkings are described in chapter 13 of volume 1.) The commanding officer of Fort Burnside, Lieutenant Colonel I. Henry Stern, was on duty in the HECP operations room at the time and authorized vessels in the area to detect, engage and attack the enemy submarine.

In April 1942, the USS *Capella*, an AKA-type transport ship, while off of Jamestown was accidentally torpedoed by a PT boat from Melville. The

HECP, aware of the explosion but not of its cause or location, set an attack condition throughout the defended seacoast area until the navy determined the origin of the torpedo and notified the HECP. The ship, which began to sink, had cargo on deck, including aircraft, but was towed by tugboats into Jamestown's Potters Cove. There, the damaged vessel grounded and heeled over on the beach. The *Capella* was later repaired and returned to service.

In another incident, the navy underwater loop system in the East Passage detected an unknown underwater object entering the bay. The HECP and other harbor defenses issued a full alert. Passes were canceled, mines activated and guns manned. The use of depth charges was forbidden in order to prevent damage to the nets and minefield. Nothing was discovered, except the next day the loop system detected an object leaving the area. Subchasers and PBY aircraft from Quonset "pummeled" the bay's bottom with depth charges and bombs, but the only result was to release odorous brown gases that emanated from an old City of Newport dumping ground.

The enemy knew that American harbors had defensive systems, even if information about exact deployments and technological developments was kept secret. It is not known to what extent knowledge of Fort Burnside's HECP and its associated coastal defense weapon systems deterred German military strategists. Nonetheless, hundreds of military personnel spent endless vigils dedicated to the unglamorous task of manning the HECP and other posts on Narragansett Bay.

On June 27, 1945, after Germany's surrender but before Japan's surrender, the HECP at Beavertail ceased operation. Fort Burnside commenced operation under U.S. Navy control in the HECP building as the Beavertail Signal Station. As the Cold War with the Soviet Union progressed, in March 1964, a naval communications transmitter site utilized all of the prior Fort Burnside grounds. A sister receiving station was located eight miles away on Sachuest Point, Middletown. In 1974, the navy consolidated and moved its communications facilities elsewhere. On April 16, 1980, all military operations were terminated, and the former Fort Burnside was deeded to the State of Rhode Island. The entire Fort Burnside site is now known as Beavertail State Park.

By the end of World War II, new tactics, weapons and technological advances eliminated the need for HECPs and fortified gun batteries. Coastal and harbor defense was outdated, and most facilities were dismantled, abandoned or destroyed. The HECP building remains, as do a few other remnants on Conanicut Island, as a unique reminder of Beavertail's contribution to the defense of Narragansett Bay during World War II.

13

Beavertail's Top Secret Spraycliff Observatory and Charlestown's Brash Night Fighters

By Varoujan Karentz

Spraycliff Observatory, located on the Beavertail peninsula on Conanicut Island (the town of Jamestown), was a top-secret World War II facility. Its activities provided a critical contribution to winning the war in the Pacific: the development of airborne radar systems to help navy combat aircraft shoot down Japanese bombers and fighters attacking at night. At Charlestown's nearby Naval Auxiliary Air Facility (NAAF), the nation's most important night fighter training facility, pilots trained using the newly developed radar, preparing to be sent to the Pacific.

During World War II, little was known of the highly classified activities at Spraycliff. Even today, original sources on its activities are limited to a few archived logbooks and progress reports.

The Japan military responded to U.S. successes in 1942 and 1943 with retaliatory attacks by bombers whose pilots preferred operating at night. Somehow Japanese airmen were effective flying at night, but U.S. Navy flyers defending against them were not. Successful nighttime attacks on American ground units and ships by Japanese light and heavy bombers escorted by fighter aircraft jolted the U.S. Navy to design, equip and train squadrons of night fighter interceptor aircraft.

By 1944 and 1945, realizing that it was beginning to lose the war, Japan launched a terrifying campaign of kamikaze aircraft against U.S. Navy aircraft carriers and other large warships. Many of these suicide attacks occurred at night. Suddenly, the need for the U.S. Navy pilots and their aircraft to excel at night fighting became a top priority. The solution was to develop an airborne radar for fighter aircraft and to train pilots how to use it.

The navy teamed up with MIT to address radar design issues and test airborne night fighting radar systems. Called Project Affirm, the highly classified military project involved a large civilian commitment of top engineers and scientists from both universities and manufacturers of military electronic equipment. The radar systems developed at Spraycliff Observatory were sent, along with a cadre of specially trained navy pilots from the NAAF Charlestown, to aircraft carriers in the Pacific. They worked with radar-equipped Combat Information Center (CIC) personnel onboard the carriers. These radar-equipped night fighters dramatically improved the combat effectiveness of navy interceptors in night battles and contributed to the U.S. victory in the Pacific.

In early 1943, on Jamestown, slightly more than a half mile to the north of the Beavertail Lighthouse, on the west side of Beavertail Road and within the confines of Fort Burnside (see prior chapter), construction of the navy's Spraycliff Observatory development and test facility was completed. Spraycliff's activities were so secret that the exact date it was established is not certain. Its work developing high-frequency radar technology was given the security code name Mickey.

While Beavertail's remote location and proximity to MIT were likely factors in locating Spraycliff Observatory at Beavertail, the primary factor probably was because of its proximity to Naval Air Station Quonset Point, the largest naval air station in the Northeast. The first night fighter unit was established at NAS Quonset Point in January 1942. Needing more room, night fighter training was transferred to NAAF Charlestown at the southern coast of Rhode Island in late 1943. Radar arrived at Charlestown in April 1944. Late in 1944, NAAF Charlestown became the main night fighter training facility on the East Coast. It housed a small ground-controlled radar facility called Cousin that was used to train radar personnel for flight squadron carrier duty.

The story of radar in the United States started in Great Britain, where it was developed. After war broke out in Europe in 1939, President Franklin D. Roosevelt and Prime Minister Winston Churchill quickly agreed that both nations should pool their technical secrets in order to develop urgently needed technologies vital to the war effort (even though the United States would not enter the war until more than a year later). Ground-based radar detection and tracking systems helped Britain win the Battle of Britain against German airpower in 1941.

Spraycliff Observatory in October 1945, in a rare photograph showing its World War II operations. *Bureau of Aeronautics Library*.

Radar, an acronym derived from the radio detection and ranging, is a system that uses the radio waves portion of the electromagnetic spectrum to detect and locate objects accurately at long ranges. Radar detection of an object occurs when it intercepts a radio wave transmission, reflecting a portion of the wave, which is processed by the radar's receiver. Materials that reflect radio waves can be detected day or night and in any kind of weather conditions. A radar system can determine such information as the range to the target, and the angular coordinates such as azimuth and altitude.

Early radar systems operated in the very high frequency (VHF) range, but the equipment was bulky and offered limited information. After the British built a successful microwave cavity magnetron, the key component in higher resolution radar systems, and shared the information with its new ally in September 1940, engineers and scientists in the United States began designing and improving their own radar systems. The British, with superior transmitters, and the United States, with the best receivers, soon began collaborating on microwave research and development.

The U.S. War Department teamed up with the nation's most knowledgeable scientific researchers working with radar at MIT. MIT formed a focused subgroup called the MIT Radiation Laboratory, commonly called RadLab, whose scientists concentrated in designing and developing the fledgling ground-based shipboard and airborne radar technology. Heavily funded by the federal government, RadLab conducted activities from October 1940 until December 1945.

The federal government contracted with American companies to produce radar equipment that was both small and light enough to be used in aircraft. Most of the microwave radars used by the United States during World War II were manufactured by companies such as Sperry, General Electric, Raytheon, RCA, Bell Laboratories/Western Electric and Westinghouse.

During the early phase of the war, RadLab's top priority was to develop a 10-centimeter microwave airborne intercept (AI) detection system. The AI airborne radar was to be installed on fighter aircraft, both aircraft carrier– and land-based, to detect, seek and destroy enemy aircraft or surface vessels during nighttime operations.

While radar component and systems engineering design were performed in Cambridge, tests, evaluation and modifications were conducted at field locations. RadLab operated field stations at East Boston (Logan Airport); Deer Island (Boston Harbor); South Dartmouth, Massachusetts; Orlando, Florida; and Beavertail in Rhode Island.

The Spraycliff site was the most visible military facility at Beavertail. With five radar towers and a stark rectangular building, called the Systems Research Field Station, as well as a dozen ancillary buildings, its military mission was obvious.

Six British engineers, some of the first developers of radar, were attached to the Mickey site at Beavertail to convey radar technology to American scientists and to solve mutual design and development problems. In turn, the British engineers sent information they learned at Spraycliff back to Britain.

The first radar on aircraft worked as follows. A radio compass site, constructed north of Spraycliff's main building, used a low-frequency, low-power transmitter and directional antennas to provide a radio beacon for incoming aircraft. Aircraft with radar equipment installed, conducting nighttime tests, would approach Spraycliff from the south over water and home in on the radio compass, enabling the pilots to fly their planes directly over Spraycliff's radars and tracking instruments.

Spraycliff contained multiple ground-based radar systems, including search, tracking and height-finding radars. The combination of these radars adapted to operational systems enabled highly accurate tracking of enemy aircraft during night operations. This development in turn led to testing of nighttime fighter aircraft operations, enabling pilots to become familiar with using aircraft-mounted radars.

A second radio compass station, operating on a different frequency, was located at the northern tip of Conanicut Island. This station helped aviators to make safe landing approaches onto the airfield at NAS Quonset Point, located just two miles to the north.

In 1942, RadLab began work on its first airborne radar design called the ASD radar. It was a 3-centimeter system (higher target resolution than the earlier 10-centimeter system) that could be installed in TBF Avenger aircraft as a surface search radar. It excelled in finding enemy submarines that had surfaced and other warships at ranges of up to 25 miles. For this special role, the TBF Avenger, flying off an aircraft carrier, used a crew of three, one serving as the radar operator.

Early in the war, the navy developed a new tactic using a TBF Avenger torpedo/dive bomber with a RadLab ASD radar installed onboard to act as a nighttime low altitude airborne controller for two fighter aircraft flying nearby, either F4F Wildcats or F4U Corsairs. The fighter aircraft directed by the TBF Avenger's three-man crew would be directed to the enemy aircraft, coming close enough to view the engine exhaust flames before engaging the enemy.

The Avenger's slow speed (cruising at 145 miles per hour, with a maximum speed of about 250) meant that the Wildcats and Corsairs often could not maintain radar contact with enemy aircraft. The urgent request for fast night-fighting single-seat aircraft equipped with small lightweight radars was passed on to MIT's RadLab. The radar equipment's size precluded it from being installed inside the aircraft. Further design work resulted in placing the radar in an external nacelle (pod) under the aircraft's starboard wing.

Originally, F4U Corsairs—fighter aircraft equipped with primitive air interception radar sets built by MIT engineers—were used in tests. In 1943, the newly developed Grumman F6F Hellcat emerged as the preferred night fighter; it was faster, easier to land and more stable as a gun platform than the Corsairs. Hellcats produced for night fighting were called F6F-5Ns—the N stood for night fighter. They were first equipped with radar at NAAF Charlestown in April 1944.

A new radar system, called AN/APS-4, was developed with three distinct functions. The first was to search for enemy aircraft and surface vessels in darkness or fog. The search position had selectable ranges of 65, 25 and 1 miles, but its operational range for picking up enemy aircraft was about 4 miles. A second function was for aiming the aircraft's guns automatically to fire on enemy aircraft. The gun aim position switch was thrown when the target was within a half mile (about 1,000 yards). When in range of 250 yards, the pilot was able to train his guns accurately on the target. The third function was to locate carrier, land or airborne beacon stations. In the beacon position, the AN/APS-4 interacted with the carrier's or land-based field's airborne beacon stations, enabling aircraft to land safely at night. The AN/APS-4 unit, weighing 180 pounds, was mounted in a pod on the F6F-5N's outer starboard wing.

Developments in radar technology by 1944 resulted in an updated and simplified radar called the AN/APS-6. It operated with only six knobs but still weighed 250 pounds. It had an aircraft search range of five and a half miles and could detect ships moving ten miles away. The display featured a double-target system that showed two blips on the screen, one for the enemy plane and the other indicating the altitude of the Hellcat relative to the target. It used a small 2-inch diameter display as the gun sight.

Early ground-based radar systems, such as the SCR 270 and 271, provided azimuth (bearing) and range on targets, but lacked the ability to determine the altitude of airborne targets. Dr. Ernest Pollard, one of RadLab's leading scientists, frequently visited Spraycliff and undertook the development of a system called the AN/CPS-4 height finder radar. He had built an experimental model for testing and evaluation at Beavertail. The land-based radar at Spraycliff had a range of ninety miles, using a twenty-five-foot antenna operated in the S-Band (2–4 GHz). It was nicknamed the Beaver Tail. The CPS-4 was successfully used by controllers at Spraycliff along with SCR 270-271 radar sets to vector the night-fighting aircraft flying from Quonset Point and Charlestown during intercept training flights.

NAAF Charlestown became the East Coast's main base for forming and training F6F-5(N) night-fighter squadrons using the various radar systems developed at Spraycliff and guided by Spraycliff personnel. It was dangerous work for pilots. A memorial erected at the former Charlestown airfield indicates that seventeen pilots in night-fighter units were killed in training accidents in 1944 and 1945. Nonetheless, under the guidance of Commander William E.G. Taylor, the night-fighter pilots developed into an elite corps of flyers. Similar training occurred at the Naval Auxiliary Air Field at Westerly.

In April 1945, a U.S. Navy's public relations office tried to describe the challenges faced by Charlestown-trained pilots flying at night against an unseen enemy without mentioning the top-secret radar they used:

Carefully chosen for flying ability, gunnery, neuro-muscular coordination, mental acuity, and personality, the cream of the Navy's exceptional fliers

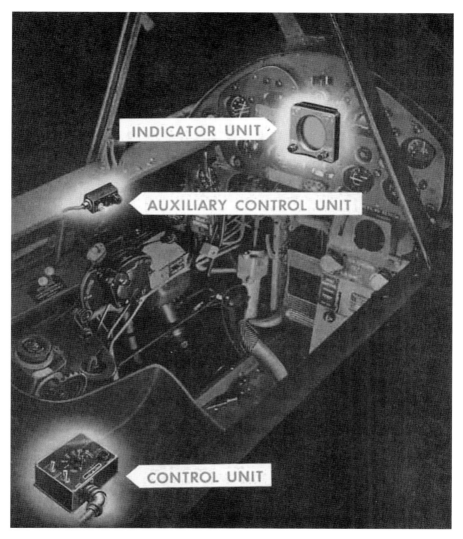

Location of radar controls on the instrument panel of a Hellcat modified for night fighting. *U.S. Navy Pilot's Operating Manual for Night Fighters, February. 17, 1944.*

are sent to the Night Fighter Training Center at the U.S. Naval Auxiliary Air Facility at Charlestown, R.I. Destined to fly from carrier decks and to fight and patrol while weary…they must operate under the most harrowing circumstances: blacked-out [aircraft carrier] *decks, poor or nonexistent visual aide, and the difficulty of distinguishing between friend and foe in total darkness.*

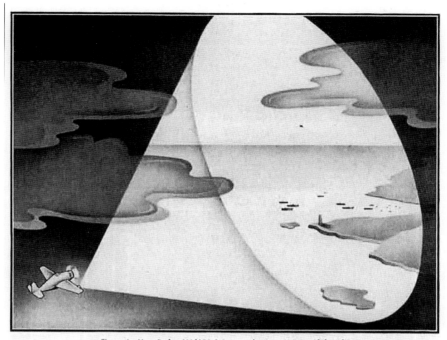

Figure 4—How Radar AN/APS-6 Sweeps the Area in Front of the Pilot

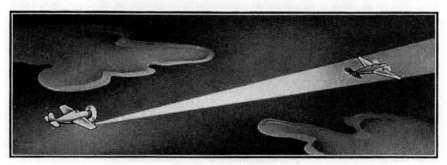

Figure 5—15° Gun Aim Scan

The two modes of the APS-6 Radar are shown in these once confidential images. The antenna beam width in the spiral scan mode was a 120-degree cone. In the conical scan (aim and shoot) mode, it was manually switched by the pilot into the narrow 15-degree cone. *U.S. Navy Pilot's Operating Manual for Night Fighters, February 17, 1944.*

Night-fighter pilots had to wear oxygen masks on all night flights and prepared for night flying by wearing red goggles for at least thirty minutes prior to taking off.

Some 1,500 Hellcats with night-flying capabilities were produced in the war, and they proved to be both an effective deterrent against nighttime Japanese attacks and a productive offensive weapon. When a Hellcat shot down a Japanese plane at night on October 25, 1944, Admiral William "Bull" Halsey credited it with saving his fleet from a kamikaze attack.

In August 2003, three surviving Hellcat pilots (Fred Dungan, Paul Kepple and John Gilman) and one electronics officer (Archie Stockebrand), members of Squadron VF(N)-76, were invited by the Jamestown Historical Society to visit Beavertail. The four men, with their modified aircraft, had been assigned to three aircraft carriers operating in the Pacific, the USS *Yorktown*, USS *Lexington* and USS *Hornet*. Not only did they train other F6F carrier pilots in the use of radar, they also participated in extensive combat operations. They saw combat from January to September 1944.

The following is a transcript of most of the interview of the four men. (Listening to the recorded interview, it is not possible to identify with certainty who is speaking; the author recalls that most of the comments were made by Fred Dungan, with Archie Stockebrand chiming in from time to time. Dungan was credited with ten enemy aircraft shot down during the war.)

Beavertail had a ground radar that directed us in the air to the bogey [the simulated enemy] *and then we would come within sight, they would pull us into the back of the target and then we would say, "Tally Ho!" and we would have the target in our radar scope and we would close in on him.*

We had two little dots on the radar scope. The right-hand dot would indicate whether the target was below us or above us so we could match his [the target's] *altitude and they would give us his speed, his estimated speed, and then we would add another fifty miles per hour to that and closing fast and then when we got to within a mile or two we'd slow down and match his speed and check the airspeed indicator to know exactly how fast we were going and then we'd close in* [on the target] *at ten or fifteen miles an hour faster.*

During the last quarter of a mile, if the radar wouldn't pick up the target you'd be in your cockpit looking for stars to be obliterated, for exhaust pipe glow to appear, for anything. And your imagination would start working.... *Finally you'd actually see something blocking out the stars. And if there were no stars you'd pick up the exhaust pipes, the little glow, and sneak*

Three pilots, one in a flight jacket, listen to an instructor using a large-scale topographical model at Charlestown. The navy's caption reads: "In the shadowy night briefing room an instructor teaches night fighter pilots how to select the best target as they wing over an objective." *National Archives*.

Night fighter pilots at Charlestown from Squadron VF(N)-108, late summer or early fall, 1944. According to the Charlestown Historical Society, only one man in the front row survived the war. George K. Kraus, kneeling in the front row on the far right, flying out of Charlestown on a night fighter training mission on October 19, 1944, was killed in an airplane crash over Preston, Connecticut. *Charlestown Historical Society*.

up on this target, visually identify it, drop back one thousand feet and your night gun sight would indicate how far back you were.

You had to know the size of the airplane, and then you would relate that on your radar scope and you'd touch your trigger and your six fifty-calibers [guns] would fire at six hundred rounds per minute and that's all it would take to eliminate that target.

Mickey fed us beautifully. These crazy flight directors were in this dark room watching the radar scope looking at blips on a chart and directing, and we had to try to direct too, and that was so difficult.... [A] target is moving say about 180 knots, going in one direction, and you are trying to direct a fighter plane that is going about 180 knots in back of him and turn him to face so that his radar will pick up at within three miles, actually five miles. You would [eventually] pick up the target. Beyond five miles we couldn't pick him up. But at three miles he'd be a very strong target.

It's hard for me to visualize any serious formal training because in Project Affirm we all did it to the best of our ability, the only way you could, which was to follow the guy in front of you and to try to shoot him down, close in. But the training syllabus was established later and, what would it take, three months?

Well, we arrived [at Charlestown] *in September of '43 and took off for Hawaii in January of '44. So that was four months. And we left two months early, because they* [navy commanders in the Pacific theater] *were getting nervous out there. They needed night fighters. The Japanese were destroying our efficiency by keeping the fleet awake at night.*

In November, we lost Butch O'Hare on a night fighter strike team. The night fighter strike team at that time was made up of a torpedo plane [a TBF/TBM Avenger] *that had big radar on it to close in on the target, and the fighter plane had the gun platform to shoot the target down. O'Hare got shot down by one of his own people. So they canceled that program.*[*]

They didn't know what to do with us. Admiral Mitchell didn't think the night fighters could fly at night or land at night. None of the skippers of the carriers had had any good experience at night. They'd all had night experience and lost people. Crashing into the island, crashing on landing, losing them by disappearing, engine malfunctions on takeoff.

---

[*] On November 26, 1943, Butch O'Hare, flying an unmodified F6F-3 on a night mission with a TBF Avenger, disappeared over the Gilbert Islands. O'Hare Field in Chicago was named after him.

The group I was with, the five pilots, ended up on the Yorktown.
The Yorktown *was skippered by Jocko Clark* [Joseph J. Clark], *a
full-blooded Cherokee Indian, the first Native American to graduate from
Annapolis. He said to our skipper Russ Reiser, "I want you on the flight
deck after supper to walk with me."…His first comment to Russ Reiser
was, "Welcome aboard Lieutenant Reiser. Now, just what the hell can you
night fighters do that those day fighters can't do?" He considered himself
a day fighter. Well, Russ went on to tell him how we can sneak up behind
them and shoot them down without them even seeing us and get back to
carrier and land very nicely and have a nice sleep all night. Russ said
Jocko Clarke's face started to beam like he had found a new toy to play
with—night fighters.*

Jocko Clarke wrote a book, an autobiography, entitled Carrier
Admiral. *In that book it was stated that Jocko Clarke turned the aircraft
carrier from a defensive mechanism to an offensive mechanism. This was
what he was thinking of: "How can I use this new tool I've got…oh
goody…we can harass the Japs at night which we used to do."…The
first time we flew at night, it was about two weeks after we got aboard
the carrier. All four went up and all four came back. We'd done it so often
it was nothing. The day fighters wouldn't even talk to us, they were so
jealous—a little professional jealousy there. We were known as "Jocko's
boys," those night fighters.*

When we transferred to the Hornet *and Jocko called for us, then it
really became a little touchy in the Ready Room. We were with the day
fighters, and we…were ostracized. So then we found room in the torpedo
squadron's Ready Room, and we went there. And they loved to have us
there. It was great, really nice. A little jealousy there, you know, because we
were so highly trained.*

*This was one thing Russ said, "Jocko, you must realize that we are
trained at the peak of our profession, of our ability, like Olympic athletes.
We have to fly a lot to maintain that proficiency." Jocko said, "I'll see
to that." That evening, he got back to his cabin and he told the air group
commander and said, "We've got these crazy night fighters aboard that have
to fly a lot to maintain their proficiency." The commander* [in turn] *told
the fighter skipper, "We've got these crazy guys who fly at night and they
need a lot of practice during the daytime to maintain their night proficiency."
And the day fighter skipper said, "I'll use them on every strike I can use
them except number one strike." Number one strike is usually when you
have shot them down. Number two strike came into a clean field. But it*

Two Grumman F6F-5N Hellcats, each with AN/APS-6 radar nacelle containing radar equipment developed at Spraycliff Observatory on its starboard wing, on the deck of the USS *Lexington* wait for action off Saipan. The planes are from Squadron VF(N)-76, to which belonged the four crewmembers interviewed in this chapter. *National Archives.*

didn't work that way. Number one strike would go into a target, he'd wake the enemy up. Number two strike, which we would be among, flying day fighters, would come in, shoot down some airplanes and come back. That's why the five of us shot down twenty-seven aircraft. And this didn't set very well with the day fighters either.

We had the training flying up against the Japanese Zero. The Japanese Zero was a much better airplane than the Hellcat….It was, under certain conditions [but] *you kept those conditions in your favor when you were flying a Hellcat, which was slow. Keep it slow. At high speed, we had such bulk and such weight that it would take us a long time to get that airplane maneuvered around. And every maneuver you make in an airplane is a parabolic maneuver. It has a start and an end, and you can pretty well predict where that end is going to be unless something violent happens in the middle of a maneuver. At slow flight, the Hellcat, you can kick the rudder around and change direction, which the Japanese couldn't do because their aircraft was that much more delicate. It wasn't as beefy. It would tear the wings off of it if they tried that. Plus we had the horsepower to pull us from a dead stall right up into a climb. That they didn't have. So we had advantages that you could use for yourself and make the Japanese look a little sick, and* [you could] *come back. Because only one person comes back from the dog fight.*

The same surface and air search radars developed at Spraycliff for training Project Affirm pilots were used to train the navy's aircraft carrier Combat Information Center (CIC) crews, who managed the vital command, control, communication and surveillance operations aboard aircraft carriers.

Dr. Ernest Pollard's AN/CPS-4 height finder radar was also used by antiaircraft air defense batteries. Edward Fazio of Westerly recalled his father telling him that he served in the army at a gun emplacement in southeastern Massachusetts that had an antiaircraft gun and radar that was connected to a searchlight. For training, he and his crew would track an incoming American warplane pretending to be an enemy aircraft. Invariably, the radar would result in the searchlight turning on and homing in on the incoming plane. (The CPS-4 went on to be used as a mainstay height finder by the U.S Army Air Defense Command worldwide for many years after the war and was also used as a precision air traffic ground control approach radar.)

Pollard, for his work on radar development, received the President's Certificate of Merit from President Harry Truman. As a result of this award, his role at Spraycliff was disclosed. The identities of most other scientists and others toiling away at Spraycliff during the war were never revealed.

RadLab engineers also developed long-range navigation (LORAN), the world's first radio navigation system prior to GPS. LORAN was spectacularly successful, with uses in both military and civilian applications. It remained the most widely used long-range navigation system for both vessels at sea and aircraft until 2010.

After war's end, the laboratories, equipment, buildings and antennas at Spraycliff were dismantled and moved or destroyed. The site of the former observatory, now part of Beavertail State Park, is overgrown with trees and shrubs. What little remains of it includes some deteriorated asphalt roads, unidentifiable metal parts, coaxial cable remnants, concrete mounting structures, antenna guy wire anchors and a concrete water cistern (see chapter 18 for directions to the site). These are the only physical remains of Spraycliff's significant contribution to the United States' victory in the Pacific theater of war.

Edward Swain Hope, the Navy's First Black Lieutenant, Trains at Davisville

By Christian McBurney

Edward Swain Hope's courage came from joining the navy as one of its first African American officers. He rose to become the highest-ranking black officer in the U.S. Navy.

Reflecting the prevailing racial prejudices of the times, the army and navy in World War II as a matter of policy discriminated against blacks on account of their color. Black sailors were restricted mostly to working as stewards aboard ships or manual laborers ashore. Military housing was segregated. By April 15, 1945, for example, the Naval Air Station at Quonset Point had built separate housing for 7,789 male sailors and other white men, 448 white women (mostly WAVES), 870 white male officers—and 838 black men. Note the lack of reference to black women—they were excluded from the WAVES until October 1944. Dances at Quonset Point were segregated, as were sports teams (except for boxing).

Joseph Stiles was interviewed about his World War II experiences as a black man. His family hailed originally from rural southern Virginia but then moved to near Freehold, New Jersey. Stiles enlisted in the navy in November 1942, as soon as he turned eighteen years old. After training at Quonset Point for nine weeks, he was sent to the Navy Auxiliary Air Facility on Martha's Vineyard. He suffered the usual prejudice as a black sailor. As were many African American enlistees, he was made a steward's mate. He served food to pilots and other officers, a few of whom acted as if he was not there. Stiles recalled the separate and unequal housing. He and seventeen other black sailors were consigned to a single Quonset hut. It was warm enough and had decent bunk beds, but they had to walk outside in the cold to get to their showers. Meanwhile, the white sailors were "in barracks, nice warm barracks," that had "showers, and everything." Unfortunately for Stiles and other black sailors at the Martha's Vineyard base, a unit of airplane mechanics included a small group of virulent white racists. On nighttime bus rides from Edgartown back to the base after liberty, drunken white soldiers from this unit sometimes tried to throw the black sailors off the bus. Stiles and six other black sailors stuck together to defend themselves. Stiles recalled that the attacks got so bad that some black sailors "were scared to go out on liberty at night. The only time they would go on liberty [was] during the day." "[T]he base got so bad that we couldn't eat at the same table they would when we'd go for chow," continued Stiles. Matters improved for the black sailors. A new base commander arrived who soon recognized the situation. He shipped out the mechanics unit and placed the black sailors in barracks. Stiles then sought a more active position. He served on a destroyer that patrolled the East Coast, with Newport and Norfolk as its main ports of call. "I went to damage control, lifesaving, and firefighting" schools, Stiles recalled. He was trained to operate and fire an antiaircraft gun. He said that open prejudice was not permitted onboard a ship, and that instead everyone worked together to defeat the enemy. After he left the U.S. Navy in 1948, appreciating the tolerant attitudes of Martha's Vineyard residents, he stayed on the island for the remainder of his life.

Edward Swain Hope, born in Atlanta, Georgia, was the son of a Brown University graduate who became the first president of Morehouse College. The son positioned himself to break down racial barriers. After receiving his undergraduate degree from Morehouse, he earned two advanced degrees in civil engineering from the Massachusetts Institute of Technology and a doctorate in personnel administration from Columbia University. He spent three years in South America working on hydroelectric development for American companies. In 1932, he had become superintendent of buildings and grounds at Howard University.

During the war, the navy began to take small steps toward integration by training a handful of black commissioned officers. Thirteen of them graduated from Officer Candidate School at Great Lakes, Illinois, in March 1944.

Two months later, the navy announced a program for the selection of ten black staff officers in the Naval Reserve, two of them in the Civil Engineer Corps. At home one night, Hope read the announcement. Living comfortably with his wife, Marion, and two children, and at age forty-two too old to be drafted, Hope nonetheless was inspired by this opportunity to be a trailblazer. He volunteered for the naval service. He passed the physical, except that he wore glasses and did not have 20-20 vision—he was given a waiver for that. On May 15, Hope was sworn in as a lieutenant junior grade, becoming the first black man to hold that rank in the navy's history.

Five days later, Hope started at the Civil Engineer Corps Officer School (also called indoctrination school) at Camp Endicott in Davisville, Rhode Island, the home of the Naval Construction Training Center for the Seabees (see chapter 4 in volume 1).

The *Pittsburgh Courier*, one of the nation's leading black-owned newspapers, sent a reporter to interview Hope at Camp Endicott in July 1944. Asked why he joined the navy, Hope responded, "Negroes ought to enter new fields, take advantage of new opportunities....And if a man

"Edward Swain Hope is sworn in as Lieutenant, CEC-V(S), USNR, at Washington, D.C. on May 15, 1944....Lieutenant Hope is the first Negro to hold the rank of Lieutenant in the Navy....He has been ordered to proceed to U.S. Naval Construction Training Center at Davisville, Rhode Island, for introduction and assignment to duty on the station force in connection with Seabee training." *New York Public Library.*

is equipped for a job that isn't usually allotted to Negroes, it's his duty to get out and get that job." Hope admitted, "My wife and I spent some time figuring out how we and the two boys could get along on a junior grade salary. We finally decided we could, and I filed the initial papers." The white personnel officer who sat in for the interview, referring to the demanding twelve-week course of study at the indoctrination school, said that "Lieutenant Hope is near the top of his class." The officer added that Hope "is carrying a burden and carrying it well."

Hope apparently did not suffer from segregation at Davisville. Along with white officers training, Hope lived in a two-story barrack and slept in a double-decker bunk bed. He complimented the food and recreational facilities at the station. The reporter observed, "He is not being given the silent treatment. He is not being patronized.…[H]e is primarily a naval officer, nothing more, nothing less."

Hope completed indoctrination school in September. He and his family moved into a house in Wakefield while he awaited orders. Meanwhile, the *Providence Journal* interviewed him for an October 8 article that detailed both his achievements and those of his distinguished father, John Hope, who was described as "an illustrious alumnus of Brown University and a leader in the advancement of his race." In the graduation ceremony for 1894, John Hope was asked by his Brown classmates to give the class speech. He did so well that he was invited to work as a reporter for the *Providence Journal*, but he declined, preferring to move back to segregated Georgia to help promote racial progress there. He served as president of Morehouse College from 1906 to 1931 and of Atlanta University from 1929 to 1936, the year he died. A Liberty ship was named for John Hope. The article added that "a community center here [in Providence] named for him has entertained 60,000 Negro servicemen since it opened in January, 1942." Black soldiers and sailors had to use segregated recreational facilities during the war. Founded in 1929 and located in Providence's West End, the John Hope Community Center was renamed, and remains today, the John Hope Settlement House.

After Hope's son graduated from indoctrination school, the Navy Department had to decide what to do with Edward Swain Hope. The navy brass was not yet ready to have a black officer on a confined ship at sea ordering around white sailors and lower-ranking officers, many of whom came from the segregated South or were prejudiced. Hope was assigned to the Manana Barracks at Pearl Harbor as a public works officer, supervising mostly black stevedores.

In December 1945, Hope became the first black naval officer to serve as a member of a general court-martial board. In January 1946, after his promotion to lieutenant commander (once again becoming the highest-ranking black navy officer), he was appointed director of instruction at Navy Pacific University in Hawaii, where he was joined by his family. After the navy closed the university later in the year, Hope was transferred to the mainland to sign his separation papers near Washington, D.C. Before he did, he was ordered to report to Secretary of the Navy James Forrestal, who asked him to remain in the navy. Hope was determined to renew his civilian career, but he informed Forrestal that he was willing to do whatever he could to encourage young black men to seek careers as navy officers. Hope agreed to go on a speaking tour to black colleges.

Hope was finally released from active duty in February 1947. (In 1948, President Truman issued his bold order integrating the armed forces.) Hope returned to Howard University, where he was appointed professor of civil engineering, while also serving as a Naval Reserve officer assigned to recruiting officer candidates of color. He remained active in the Naval Reserve until the 1950s. He later became chairman of the civil engineering department at the American University in Beirut, Lebanon. In 1956, he wrote a letter to Martin Luther King supporting his Montgomery, Alabama boycott. Hope noted that the Arabic press in the Middle East made frequent and "considerable mention" of it. He also enclosed a $100 donation.

Could *U-853*'s Sinking of *Black Point* Have Been Averted?

By Christian McBurney

In 2010, John G. Bradley, Jr., a former pilot raised in Hartford, Connecticut, told a remarkable story about the German U-boat *U-853*. This U-boat sank the coal collier *Black Point* on May 5, 1945, south of Point Judith and hours later was itself attacked and went down within sight of Point Judith (see volume 1, chapter 13). The following is based on the 2010 interview (available on YouTube) and my 2018 interview with Bradley at the Wickford Yacht Club, where, at age ninety-four, he still moored his sailboat.

Early in the morning of May 5, 1945, with Germany's surrender just two days away, Ensign John Bradley and his temporary radioman, Clifford I. Brinson, took off from NAS Quonset Point and flew their TBM Avenger to a designated point in Long Island Sound, south of New London, Connecticut. Bradley's orders were to help train the crew of a submarine operating out of Groton to spot approaching enemy aircraft. In World War II, submarines operated by battery power underwater and diesel power on the surface. Submarines regularly had to surface to recharge their batteries, making them vulnerable to enemy aircraft. Bradley was directed to fly out to the submarine's horizon and then fly back to the submarine from random directions so that lookouts on the submarine's conning tower could try to spot his approaching plane. With fog rolling in, the training exercise ended at 10:15 a.m.

Bradley then flew his Avenger ten miles south of Fisher's Island and turned east toward Block Island, patrolling his assigned sector. Suddenly, Brinson

PBY-5A seaplanes fly over the air control tower at Naval Air Station Quonset Point, February 13, 1943. If John Bradley had immediately radioed in his sighting of *U-853* to Quonset, planes such as these could have been sent against *U-853*. Whether they would have been in time to save *Black Point* is not clear. Bradley recalled he was not allowed to use his radio with the German submarine nearby. It was also a foggy day. The core of the former air control tower still exists. *National Archives.*

turned to his pilot and said, "Mr. Bradley, I can't believe my eyes. There is a German submarine just east of Montauk, Long Island." Bradley looked over and saw it. They could tell it was a U-boat because of its distinctive "laundry-basket" conning tower and angular hull of a type IX-C U-boat. Its commander was recharging the U-boat's batteries.

Bradley lacked live weapons onboard his aircraft to attack the submarine. He recalled that he was under orders not to use his VHF radio, as it could be easily picked up by the German submarine. He thought the best chance to sink the enemy submarine was to fly back to Quonset Point and report the sighting immediately, where hunter-killer aircraft could be sent out to locate and attack the submarine (or at least scare it away). Bradley peeled off and sped at wave-top height toward Quonset, hoping the German submariners had not spotted him. Proceeding up the West Passage of Narragansett Bay in increasing fog, Bradley landed his plane on the northwest runway at Quonset Point, taxied over to a seaplane hangar and parked his aircraft. He then sprinted to the administration building to inform the commanding officer of NAS Quonset Point, Dixie Kiefer, of what he saw. Bradley met an aide outside of Kiefer's office, who assigned a Combat Information Officer (CIO) to meet with Bradley and Brinson. (Bradley thinks his name was Monaghan.)

The CIO debriefed Bradley and Brinson about the U-boat sighting. The CIO expressed skepticism, despite Bradley firmly stating, "We know what we saw, there was no question about it." Bradley added information about the U-boat's speed and direction, which would allow its eastward course to be plotted. The debriefing started at 1:00 p.m. and ended three hours later. The CIO officer occasionally left the room and returned. He must have been consulting with a superior officer (could it have been Dixie Kiefer?). Once, after returning from another such visit, the CIO said he knew that Bradley and Brinson had been out at a Providence bar until 3:00 a.m. that morning. Bradley conceded the point but said that he and Brinson did not drink. One problem was that Bradley and Brinson were new to Quonset Point. Bradley and his squadron had flown up from Norfolk, Virginia, about a week prior to May 5. On his way out, the CIO told Bradley and Brinson he would report the sighting to the headquarters of the cruiser-destroyer fleet at Newport. When Bradley went outside after the debriefing, he recalled that heavy fog had rolled in.

That evening, at about 5:40 p.m., the commander of *U-853* spotted a merchant vessel less than three miles southeast of Point Judith. It was the coal collier *Black Point*. The German submarine fired a single torpedo at it. The torpedo smashed into the vessel's stern—the ensuing explosion and vessel's sinking killed eleven crew members and one guard. Thirty-four survivors were rescued by small craft operating out of the Coast Guard Station at Point Judith and from Quonset Point. The next morning, still within sight of Point Judith, *U-853* was sunk by hedgehogs and depth charges deployed by the coast guard frigate *Moberly* and navy destroyer escort *Atherton*. All fifty-five of the U-boat's crew perished.

No evidence has appeared of Bradley's report or that it was conveyed to Newport or acted upon. Bradley still agonizes to this day whether his information, if acted upon, could have saved lives. Based on the projected course and speed of the U-boat he sighted, Bradley calculated it would have arrived off Point Judith at about the time *Black Point* was sunk. Thus, he is confident he and Brinson had spotted *U-853*. Bradley believes that even if the information had been conveyed to Newport headquarters and acted upon quickly, there was not sufficient time to send out antisubmarine warships after 4:00 p.m. on May 5 and for them to sink the enemy submarine before it attacked *Black Point* at 5:40 p.m. His assessment is correct. It appears that all of the Newport-based destroyers were on patrol at the time and not near Point Judith. It typically took hours to gather a crew and start up the engines of a heavy cruiser. In the foggy conditions, it would have been dangerous to send out hunter-killer antisubmarine aircraft from Quonset Point or Charlestown.

On the other hand, the information that an enemy submarine could be lurking in Rhode Island Sound could have been immediately radioed to commercial ships operating in Rhode Island Sound and Block Island Sound. The unsuspecting captain of *Black Point*, oblivious to the risk of a U-boat attack, did not even post lookouts or adopt the tactic of zigzagging to avoid enemy torpedoes.

A naval historian who reviewed the preceding story wrote to me: "The story sounds quite credible that Bradley's aircraft sighted *U-853*, but it is also quite credible that the crew were not believed and no action was taken. One of the most difficult things in war is to know what intelligence is correct and which of the bits of information needs to be acted upon immediately." I also found contemporary records confirming Bradley's service as a pilot trainee, Brinson's service in southern New England with an aircraft squadron and some other details consistent with Bradley's story.

Elisabeth Sheldon

HER SUMMERS OF 1944 AND 1945 ON NARRAGANSETT BAY

By Christian McBurney

Elisabeth Kellog Sheldon knew she was fortunate. Known as Betty, she enjoyed her privileged upbringing, which included attending private boarding schools and a private college. Now here she was in early June 1944, a pretty and bright twenty-year-old woman ready to spend another summer in her family's twelve-bedroom shingled house north of Saunderstown called Spindrift, with its commanding view of Narragansett Bay.

There was a lot to see in Narragansett Bay at the height of World War II. To the north stood the Naval Air Station at Quonset Point, the largest navy air base in the Northeast. Aircraft coming and going from Quonset Point roared over Spindrift incessantly. Torpedoes manufactured at Newport were tested, fired out of the end of a modified building at the tip of Gould Island and then tracked and recovered by small boats scurrying after them. Squadrons of small PT boats could be heard speeding up and down the bay. And, of course, there was a constant stream of navy warships coming in and out of the bay—mostly destroyers and destroyer escorts, but on occasion, larger ships, such as a heavy cruiser or a flat-top aircraft carrier.

It was unusual that Betty and her family were allowed to remain in Spindrift during the war. Most of the summer homes on the bay had been requisitioned for use by navy officers stationed at Quonset Point. Betty was thus lucky that her family did not have to leave Spindrift. Well, not really lucky. Her parents had recently separated, and since this was the only house her mother, Margaret Chase Sheldon (called Marjorie), had, the family was allowed to remain. For most of the year, Betty attended college at Bryn Mawr outside Philadelphia. Her two older brothers, Irving and Rhody, were already serving in the navy, and her older sister Peggy had moved to California after marrying a navy pilot who was then flying missions in the Pacific. Now it was the beginning of another warm and breezy summer on Narragansett Bay.

Betty spent much of the time with her spunky sister Louise (known as Lulu), two years younger. Both were skilled sailors, taught by their energetic father, James Rhodes Sheldon. He descended from an old Rhode Island family and insisted his young girls learn to sail just like boys. Active members of the Saunderstown Yacht Club, the Sheldon sisters loved sailing wooden fifteen-foot Lawleys. Betty's father gave her one for Christmas in 1938, named *Sirocco*, that was moored at the club.

The first thing Betty did each summer during the war was to obtain her sailing permit. Rhode Island had been declared a "vital war zone," which meant strict security measures were taken against potential spies and sabotage of military bases and war industries. Certain parts of Narragansett Bay were off-limits, particularly areas where torpedo testing occurred. When Betty obtained a permit to sail in parts of Narragansett Bay, her permit contained an ominous condition: "ENEMY ALIENS ARE PROHIBITED ON BOARD."

Photos in Betty's scrapbook, the one on the left of her holding aloft her model PBM, the one on the right with a real PBM from Quonset Point flying overhead, 1944. Betty wears a flight jacket given to her by Jim Bistodeau. *Collection of Elisabeth Kellogg Sheldon Aschman.*

Back at Spindrift, Marjorie did what she could for some of the military officers in the area, inviting them to dinners and social gatherings. She was very civic-minded and enjoyed providing a "home away from home" for the officers. Betty and Louise, as well as their friends, were also glad to extend hospitality and friendship to the officers.

A small coast guard boat, YP-15, patrolled the bay near Spindrift. Louise recalled, "We became friends and we had the crew over for a swim and a meal many times." Betty and Louise would leave a towel on a fence to alert the crew to when a cake had been baked for them.

Marjorie and her mother, Lizzie, also organized events at the nearby Dunes Club for officers at Quonset Point, who were permitted to use the club's facilities. The officers looked sharp in their dress white uniforms when they arrived at the Dunes Club. Betty and Louise would often attend club evening events, mingling and dancing with the navy pilots. The pilots hailed from all parts of the country. They missed their families and friends and welcomed the brief distraction the Sheldon sisters and their friends provided.

Naval Air Station Quonset Point had three primary missions. First, it sent out airplanes daily to search for and destroy German submarines prowling in offshore waters seeking to sink American merchant ships. Second, it trained torpedo, fighter and seaplane pilots, mostly to be sent to war in the Pacific against the Japanese. Third, it repaired and maintained aircraft, including ones that flew off aircraft carriers.

"Several of the fighter pilots we knew thought it was daring to fly under the Jamestown Bridge and a couple did," recalled Louise. "Flying under the bridge was prohibited as extremely dangerous!" she added. Louise also remembered the pilots' excitement when the new F6F Hellcat fighter plane arrived at Quonset.

Betty had an obsession with PBMs (Martin PBM Mariners) and PBYs (PBY Catalinas). They were huge reconnaissance aircraft, known as flying boats since they could take off and land on water. The word *obsession* was rarely used back then; she admitted she had been "wild about PBMs." She even had a small model PBM in her bedroom. Betty loved to hear the PBMs and PBYs roaring over her house at 7:30 in the morning on their way to antisubmarine patrols to the south. She knew that the planes would return and arrive back at Quonset Point later in the day at 3:30 p.m. She and Louise would sometimes sail their Lawleys up the bay to Quonset Point to watch the seaplanes when they returned and landed on the bay in the late afternoon. "The cascade of the water spray when the PBMs landed was beautiful," Betty fondly remembered years afterward.

After landing, the plane's thirteen crew members would crowd around the exit door, chatting with the sisters in their sailboats. No doubt they also took notice of the two-piece swimsuits the sisters wore, made by them from used jeans, which at that time was rather exotic. Louise also recalled, "My sister and I loved to sail around the moored PBYs and talk to the crews. It was a long haul back to Saunderstown against the prevailing breeze!"

Two PBM pilots, at a Dunes Club event, took an interest in the Sheldon sisters. One of them, twenty-three-year-old Jim Bistodeau from Dayton, Minnesota, became smitten with Betty. After attending the University of Minnesota, he had enlisted in the navy in June 1942. He was then commissioned a lieutenant at Corpus Christi, Texas, in September 1943, where he trained to fly planes. He arrived at Quonset Point that summer to train to fly PBMs and was one of a group of officers Marjorie had invited to social gatherings at Spindrift. His experience with PBMS piqued Betty's interest in Jim, and she liked his infectious smile—he, in turn, quickly fell for Betty.

Jim's fellow pilot, Lieutenant Otho Leonard Edwards, liked Louise. But mature as she was, Louise was still too young for a serious relationship. Like Jim, Otho had also enlisted in the navy in 1942. The four of them also palled around with another navy pilot, tall and handsome Forbes Whiteside. They all had fun together, spending as much time with one another as pilot training would allow.

Betty had to return to college. Jim's, Otho's and Forbes's training was coming to an end. Jim and Otho would fly in the same squadron of PBMs in the Pacific, VPN-27, while Forbes would initially be sent to Europe. Jim told Betty that he loved her and wanted to marry her. Betty was unsure how to respond. She was fond of Jim, of course, but she was still young and naïve, having never before had a serious relationship. But she knew that Jim would soon be far away from his family and risking his life fighting against Japan. She wanted him to be happy and have something to look forward to. She said yes to his proposal, even though deep down at the time she did not intend to abide by it. Betty was hardly the only woman during the war to make such a decision.

Betty and Jim were engaged. They talked about a ring, and in the meantime, Jim gave Betty his worn leather flight jacket. On September 5, Jim and Otho saw Betty off on a train at Kingston Station, on her way back to Bryn Mawr College.

In the evening of September 14, 1944, a tropical hurricane struck Rhode Island. Known as the Great Atlantic Hurricane of 1944, it packed powerful

Forbes Whiteside (*left*), Jim Bistodeau and fellow pilot Lester Placke (*right*) frolic at Spindrift after helping to clean damage there caused by the September 14, 1944 hurricane. *Collection of Elisabeth Kellogg Sheldon Aschman.*

winds. It was not as destructive as the hurricane of 1938 that had flattened the Dunes Club and the Coast Guard House in Narragansett and had killed more than one hundred in the state. Still, it caused considerable damage in southern New England, including dislodging a 6-inch cannon at nearby Fort Varnum. Jim, Otho and Forbes rushed over to Spindrift the next morning to help clean up the Sheldons' property. They made it a fun day.

Soon the three pilots were off to war. Betty wrote to Jim often.

In the summer of 1945, Marjorie Sheldon invited for dinner officers at Fort Kearney, located just down the road in Saunderstown, above the old ferry landing at the end of South Ferry Road. Fort Kearney was the location of a new and extraordinary prisoner-of-war camp for German soldiers. This top-secret camp was designed for anti-Nazi POWs who hated Hitler. The U.S. Army taught them about democracy, and they, in turn, published a newspaper that was distributed to some 380,000 German POWs in the United States, trying to persuade their fellow POWs to help build a democratic and tolerant postwar Germany. Even though the war with

Germany had ended with Allied victory in May 1945, it would take another year for most POWs to be repatriated back to Germany. (This special camp is the subject of chapter 11 in volume 1).

The Sheldon family soon became friends with Captain Robert L. Kunzig, the camp's commander, and Lieutenant Robert Pestalozzi, a favorite of the POWs. Both men were talented and helped make the camp at Fort Kearney a success. Betty and Louise recalled that Kunzig and Pestalozzi each spoke fluent German and enjoyed their jobs. Marjorie often invited the captain and the lieutenant to Spindrift for dinner. Afterward, they would all join in singing songs, with Kunzig pounding away at the piano and Pestalozzi playing the accordion. Sometimes, Pestalozzi, whose family hailed from Switzerland, would yodel. Everyone had fun. Once, a POW driver picked up Captain Kunzig from Spindrift; the driver was trusted enough to go outside the prison camp (recall the war with Germany had ended). Another time, the Sheldons were invited to the camp, where they were served a fine dinner cooked by the POW chef and attended by a waiter who was also a POW.

Betty continued to write letters to Jim. Once she included in the letters photographs of her in a swimsuit, pretending to be a Polynesian woman. Jim reveled in it. He also sent his fiancée a brand-new replacement leather flight jacket. But Betty had a bad premonition. Jim was flying missions in a dangerous place.

As the summer wore on, it became clear that the United States would soon win the war against Japan, ending the long nightmare that was World War II. Then all the servicemen could come back home, including, among millions of others, Jim, Otho and Forbes.

Finally, on August 15, the victory over Japan was announced. Everyone was jubilant. Marjorie held a party that evening, and she and her daughters invited over their friends. It was a grand event.

During the party, Betty was informed of an urgent telephone call for her upstairs. She rushed to the second floor. It was a Navy Department official on the phone. Jim and his PBM were missing, the voice at the other end of the line said. Jim had been piloting a PBM over Formosa on August 8, but he and his aircraft never returned. Of course, the implication was that he could be dead. Stunned, Betty put the receiver back down on the phone. A lump developed in her throat, and she felt ill. But she decided not to tell any of the party guests downstairs. She did not want to spoil their gay moods. Let them enjoy this memorable night.

Betty would learn later that both Jim and his friend Otho were killed that August 8. She pieced together what happened from a newspaper report that summarized a letter the Navy Department had sent to the parents of Otho, who had been awarded the Distinguished Flying Cross, and a letter from Forbes Whiteside. Forbes, who also received the Distinguished Flying Cross, once spent six days in a raft with his flight crew after the successful ditching of their disabled PBM. Another time, he had flown over the Japanese city of Nagasaki following the dropping of the second atomic bomb.

On that fateful night of August 8, Jim and Otho flew one PBM, and a newer (but still experienced) crew flew another. They took off from the Sakishima Islands, searching for enemy vessels supplying Japanese troops on nearby Formosa. At about 7:30 p.m., they attacked three enemy motor torpedo boats, forcing them onto a beach. They reported the incident and indicated that the two PBMs would continue their mission. No word was heard from either plane again. Eleven days later, the only trace of the missing planes was a PBM wing found floating in the water. Eventually, one of the wrecked PBMs was located in the ocean and pulled ashore. Forbes Whiteside thought that the only explanation that made sense was that the two PBMs had accidentally collided in midair. He wrote to Betty, "All the night flights were made without running lights on the planes." "The most likely conclusion that anyone has drawn," he continued, was that flying in the "pitch black the two planes collided and crashed so quickly that the radioman hadn't time to even begin a message."

All twenty-two crewmen on the two PBMs were presumed dead. It is doubtful any of their bodies were ever recovered.

The grieving Betty took some consolation sailing her boat on Narragansett Bay. That summer, she frequently took Captain Kunzig sailing. One day, Kunzig confided to her that he was nervous about an upcoming visit by Major General John Hildring, who would be inspecting Fort Kearney. If the visit went well, maybe Kunzig would be promoted. Kunzig thought it would be a grand idea if he took General Hildring sailing. He was sure the general would enjoy it. Kunzig had his own boat he could use.

Several days prior to General Hildring's inspection, Kunzig sailed to Spindrift and left his sailboat at the dock. He had dinner at the house as usual and played piano for the Sheldon family. As darkness fell, he decided to leave his boat behind and be driven back to Fort Kearney. But that night a storm kicked up and damaged Kunzig's boat. It could not be repaired in time for the day of the big inspection.

Betty felt bad that the boat was out of service and desperately wanted to help her friend, Captain Kunzig. She decided she would sail her own sailboat

A German prisoner of war at Fort Kearney drew each of the camp's last forty POWs in 1945 and accompanied each drawing with a short description of the POW in German. Here, with a pipe in his mouth, is Alfred Andersch, who would become a respected novelist in postwar years. Below him, a POW braves the ice-cold waters during the winter. *Paul Metzner, in the collection of Joachim Metzner.*

Sirocco down to Fort Kearney and let Kunzig use it to take General Hildring out for a sail. She set out in her boat from Saunderstown for the one-mile trip to the south. Back at Fort Kearney, Captain Kunzig sat with General Hildring on the porch of the captain's yellow headquarters building, both enjoying the cool breeze and spectacular view. Kunzig was then surprised to see Betty sailing down toward Fort Kearney in her Lawley. He was even more surprised, shocked actually, when Betty brought her sailboat to the dock at Fort Kearney, tied it up and dove into the bay, apparently intending to swim the one mile back to Spindrift. Worried, Kunzig called for immediate assistance, requesting a motorboat be sent to rescue Betty. But Betty knew what she was doing—she had timed her trip so that the tide would take her back up to Saunderstown.

Soon the summer of 1945 came to an end. The days of World War II, when so many contributed toward the common goal of defeating the Axis powers, were gone forever.

After graduating from Bryn Mawr with a major in chemistry, Betty became an airline stewardess, at a time when civilian flight was in its infant stage. Once during a layover in Minneapolis, Minnesota, she was invited to see Jim Bistodeau's parents. She agreed, and they could not have been nicer to her. She also received heartfelt letters from Otho Edwards's parents.

Betty married a business manager and lived many years in Hartford and then Florida. Louise became a magazine reporter in Europe and then a foreign correspondent for United Press International, spurred by her exposure to German culture in Narragansett Bay. Happily, both of them frequently visited Spindrift in the summers. Betty and her husband built a house next door to Spindrift after it was sold. In her last years, she lived in a house at Saunderstown with her older brother Irving, until she passed away in 2019 at the age of ninety-five. Louise passed away in 2018, at the age of ninety-three. Forbes Whiteside became an artist of some renown and passed away at age ninety-six in 2015.

Betty kept Jim's replacement flight jacket all these years. She wore it often, as did her children and a nephew (see a photograph of it on the back cover). Despite all the wear, Betty's repairs to the jacket and the passage of seventy-five years, one of its pockets still contains the following note from Jim Bistodeau to Betty: "Hope this is all right honey. It's a nice new one—not battle worn like the other. Love, Jim."

War Hero Dixie Kiefer's Final Bow at Quonset Point

By Christian McBurney

Dixie Kiefer, born in Blackfoot, Idaho, in 1886, graduated from the Naval Academy in June 1918. After serving in Europe during World War I, he became a navy pilot in 1922 and stayed with naval aviation.

As executive officer onboard the aircraft carrier USS *Yorktown*, Kiefer fought at the Battle of Coral Sea in early May 1942 and was awarded the Distinguished Service Medal for "exceptionally meritorious service." At the Battle of Midway on June 7, *Yorktown* was sunk by Japanese bombers. Kiefer was awarded the Navy Cross for his continued efforts trying to rescue men among the ship's raging fires, despite his falling and breaking his own foot and ankle.

Kiefer gained some celebrity status after starring in a documentary released in 1944 about the *Yorktown*, titled *The Fighting Lady*. (This documentary admiringly calls the carrier's pilots the "Knights of the Sky" and asserts most of them had been trained at Quonset Point.)

After being hospitalized and serving in several positions stateside, in May 1944, Kiefer assumed command of the newly commissioned aircraft carrier USS *Ticonderoga*. Its Air Group inflicted heavy damage on Japanese forces off Formosa on January 21, 1945. But two enemy kamikaze planes struck his ship, killing 144 sailors and injuring 200 others. Though severely hurt—with sixty-five wounds from flying shrapnel—Kiefer remained on the bridge for twelve hours, directing his heavily damaged ship from a stretcher until it was out of danger. In an unprecedented maneuver, he deliberately flooded part of his vessel, causing it to list ten degrees, so that flaming debris could slide overboard. For his service onboard *Ticonderoga*, he was awarded the Silver Star Medal.

After his recovery, on April 19, 1945, Kiefer reported for duty at Quonset Point as commander, Naval Air Bases, First Naval District (covering New England), with additional duty as commander, Naval Air Station, Quonset Point. At Quonset, Kiefer endeared himself to the officers and enlisted men by his kindly and tolerant treatment. "One regular guy," they called him, despite his war hero status. He frequently attended sporting events at Quonset and encouraged the WAVES.

Kiefer, his wrist still in a cast from battle injuries, had the pleasure of receiving official word at the Naval Air Station of the surrenders of both Germany in May 1945 and Japan in August 1945. The celebration following Kiefer's announcement of Germany's surrender was muted; everyone knew more work was needed. But the jubilation after Kiefer's announcement of Japan's unconditional surrender at 7:00 p.m. on August 19 was raucous. Commodore Kiefer, according to the *Quonset Point Scout*, "dropped in at the Waves Lounge to see how the WAVES and their guests were celebrating. No sooner had he entered the doorway when two brawny sailors hoisted him up on their shoulders. While being carried around, the crowd broke out with 'Ticonderoga'—the song written in honor of the proud carrier the Commodore commanded before coming to Quonset Point."

Commodore Dixie Kiefer in a photograph taken on June 2, 1945, as commander of NAS Quonset Point. His wrist is still in a cast from his injury suffered in action on an aircraft carrier in the Pacific. *National Archives.*

Tragically, on November 11, 1945, Commodore Kiefer's plane, headed to Quonset Point in rainy and foggy weather, crashed in mountains outside Fishkill, New York, killing Kiefer and five other officers and men from Quonset. Hearing the news, some 240 sailors and marine volunteers were bused that night to New York to search for his lost plane. On November 15, memorial services were held for Kiefer and the other five men at Quonset's auditorium, filled to capacity with mourners. The next day, Kiefer was buried with full military honors in Arlington Cemetery. The Navy Chapel at Quonset Point was named in his honor.

A Guide to World War II Sites
in Rhode Island

By Norman Desmarais and Christian McBurney

This chapter identifies existing important World War II sites in Rhode Island and what remains. If nothing from the war is left of a site, it is not included. This chapter is arranged by city/town, from north to south. Each entry gives the name, address and GPS coordinates, followed by a brief description of its activity in World War II and its present condition. All descriptions relate to World War II, unless otherwise stated. A chapter reference in the discussion (such as "see chapter 5") means see the chapter in this book for a more detailed discussion, unless the chapter reference refers to "volume 1," which refers to our first *World War II Rhode Island* book.

WOONSOCKET

Woonsocket's mills produced a variety of military products during World War II. See chapter 5.

Alice Mill, 85 Fairmount Street, 42.003774, -71.522949

The Alice Mill, once the largest rubber mill in the world when constructed in 1889, during the war employed 1,500 persons. It manufactured inflatable boats, rubber rafts, convoy balloons, barrage balloons, lifesaving suits and

Alice Mill, once the largest rubber mill in the world, burned down on June 7, 2011, leaving only the gatehouse, shown here. *Norman Desmarais.*

wading suits for launching and maintaining seaplanes. The mill produced wading suits and life jackets used in the D-Day invasion. It also made rubber tanks used by General George Patton's army as decoys. The building burned down on June 7, 2011, leaving only the gatehouse.

Jacob Finkelstein & Sons, 128 Singleton Street, 42.010850, -71.528353

Jacob Finkelstein & Sons manufactured military outerwear—trench coats, field jackets, pea coats, leather bomber jackets and rubberized rainwear. Today, most of the building is used for warehousing. Northwest Woolen Mills uses part of the building to produce woolen blankets for the Red Cross, the army and prisons.

Nyanza Manufacturing, 159 Singleton Street, 42.010039, -71.529017

The four-building complex, along with Jacob Finkelstein & Sons, were the last mills built in Woonsocket. Goodyear Fabrics Corporation leased the mill to manufacture "urgently needed equipment for the armed services." The building is now leased as business space.

Taft-Peirce Manufacturing Company, 32 Mechanic Avenue, 42.009236, -71.513061

Taft-Peirce made parts for Oerlikon-Gazda antiaircraft guns, precision tools, gauges, valves, radar equipment and torpedo parts. It employed some two thousand employees. Today, most of the large complex is used for self-storage; part of it is used by the Woonsocket Industrial and Technology Center.

SMITHFIELD

Three army servicemen were killed when their Lockheed RB-34 aircraft crashed on Wolf Hill in Georgiaville on August 5, 1943. Two memorials were constructed to honor them. The first is at Deerfield Park (*41.882066, -71.551402*), in the Greenville section of Smithfield, with the second at the crash site on Wolf Hill (*41.888438, -71.529407*) in Georgiaville.

LINCOLN

Lonsdale Mill, 195 Carrington Street, 41.909868, -71.405754

A Navy Construction Equipment Repair Depot and Navy Material Redistribution Center were located in the Lonsdale section of Lincoln, probably in the Lonsdale Mill. What little is left of the mill complex is a fabric store and artisan studios.

Pawtucket

Pawtucket hosted the Resident Inspector of Naval Material and the Navy Material Redistribution Center Annex.

Collyer Insulated Wire Co., 249 Roosevelt Avenue, 41.881280, -71.382186

Collyer Insulated Wire manufactured Resistol cables and wires, used onboard Navy and Maritime Commission ships and on army and navy aircraft. It also produced superflexible synthetic rubber-sheathed welding and locomotive gathering cables. It employed around 1,200 workers in its four plants in 1943. Today, the building is home to Rhode Island Council of Community Mental Health Organizations and Pawtucket's state Department of Human Services office.

Providence

The navy had a recruiting office on Exchange Plaza, now known as Kennedy Plaza, as well as other offices such as the Zone Intelligence Office, Navy Cost Inspector, Industry Cooperation Division, U.S. Navy Routing Office, Veterans Administration and Naval Inspector of Ordnance. Many supply ships unloaded at Providence's wharves, and the Naval Supply Depot maintained a cold storage plant in Providence. With its restaurants, bars, movie theaters and USO clubs, Providence was also the favorite place in the state for sailors and soldiers on liberty to visit.

Biltmore Hotel, 11 Dorrance Street, 41.824322, -71.413459

This attractive hotel, built in 1922, was the headquarters of Antoine Gazda and the American Oerlikon Gazda Corporation (later A. O. G. Corporation) of Providence. Gazda coordinated the work of 26 factories in Rhode Island and nearby states to produce 20-millimeter antiaircraft guns that were installed aboard most U.S. Navy warships, from PT boats to battleships. See chapter 7, volume 1. The Biltmore still operates as a hotel. Gazda operated on the tenth floor out of suite 1009, which no longer exists. During the war, the Biltmore also had a high-end restaurant and bar, which were favorite places for officers on liberty. Currently called the Graduate Providence, its interior is not as grand as it once was. The corporation rented six floors at the Cosmopolitan Building at 100 Fountain Street in Providence. Gazda also rented a building to conduct experiments at Hanson's Boat Yard at the head of Salt Pond (now in the vicinity of Stone Cove Marina at 134 Salt Pond Road in Wakefield).

Brown & Sharpe, 200-250 Promenade Street, 41.828577, -71.419339

Brown & Sharpe nearly doubled its workforce, to eleven thousand, in 1942 to produce metal machine tools and attachments, machinist tools, cutters, gray iron castings, tool blades, lathes and precision instruments such as calipers and micrometers built to fine tolerances for military uses. See chapter 7, volume 1. Today, the part of the site east of Holden Street is occupied by the University of Rhode Island's Providence campus, while the part west of Holden Street is occupied by the Rhode Island Quality Institute.

Gorham Manufacturing Company, 371 Adelaide Avenue, 41.795265, -71.430268

The Gorham Manufacturing Company switched from making high-quality sterling silverware to producing small arms parts, tank bearings, torpedo components, medals and millions of 40-millimeter shell casings. See chapter 7, volume 1 (and photograph in chapter 5 of this volume). The Providence property is now occupied by Dr. Jorge Alvarez High School and Mashapaug Commons.

Imperial Knife Company, Imperial Place, 41.816989, -71.411483

The Imperial Knife Company made military blades—knives, swords and bayonets. See chapter 7 and photograph in chapter 8, volume 1. The factory has been converted to a mix of residential and office space.

John Hope Settlement House, 7 Thomas P. Whitten Way, 41.816727, -71.425057

Named the John Hope Community Center, it hosted African American soldiers and sailors during the war. Segregated facilities were the order of the day in the military. A newspaper in 1944 reported that it "has entertained 60,000 Negro servicemen since it opened in January, 1942." Located in Providence's West End, it is today called the John Hope Settlement House.

Walsh-Kaiser Shipyard, 24 Fields Point Drive, between New York Avenue, Providence, and Narragansett Street, Cranston, 41.791836, -71.385219

The Walsh-Kaiser Shipyard (also known as Providence Shipyard) employed more than 20,000 workers at its peak and built 11 Liberty ships, 32 combat-loaded cargo ships and 21 frigates. It was the largest private employer in the state's history at one site. See chapter 7, volume 1. Remarkably, nothing remains of the formerly massive shipyard, built on filled earth extending into the Providence River. Today, the site is mainly used by Johnson and Wales University as its Harborside Campus, Save the Bay Headquarters and the Port of Providence as a bulk cargo transfer terminal.

SCITUATE

Chopmist Hill Listening Post, 183 Darby Road, 41.819760, -71.645381

The Suddard farm once housed the important Chopmist Hill Listening Post. See chapter 3. It is now a private residence. Stumps of the utility poles are still visible. The remains of an old cinderblock generator building, still surrounded with rusting chain link fencing and barbed wire, is on an adjoining neighbor's property. A blockhouse smothered in ivy stands just to the west of the house. The remains of a radio tower, with some antennae, also covered in ivy, probably date from the postwar era.

CRANSTON

A Naval Cost Inspector's office was located at Standard Machinery Co.'s office in Cranston.

Cranston Arms Company, 1655 Elmwood Avenue, 41.762331, -71.426664

The Universal Winding Company set up a new firm, the Cranston Arms Company Inc., to manufacture Johnson semiautomatic rifles and machine guns for the U.S. Marine Corps and the Dutch army. The building is now the home of Elmwood Fabric Handlers, Accent Display Corporation and Uxbridge Carvers.

WARWICK

Hillsgrove Army Air Base (Theodore Francis Green Memorial State Airport), 2190 Post Road, 41.725989, -71.435231

The U.S. Army Air Corps leased the state airport on April 1, 1942, and called it Hillsgrove Army Air Base. It became a fighter base for the First Army Air Corps and a transition-training base for officers upon graduation from flight school. Construction of Hangar No. 2 for the Rhode Island National Guard was completed in 1942. At least ten pilots died in accidental crashes of planes flying out of Hillsgrove, four flying P-47 Thunderbolts on the foggy morning of February 11, 1943. The Army Air Corps returned control of the air base to the State of Rhode Island on September 26, 1945, where it became once again Theodore Francis Green Memorial State Airport. Buildings that were used at Hillsgrove and are still being used today are on the Northwest Ramp north of Airport Road (*41.733201, -71.429627*) and include the original terminal building (now used for administrative offices) and recently improved Hangar No. 2 (49,700 square feet). Hangar No. 1, completed in 1939, was demolished in 2014.

WARREN

Warren Boat Yard, 57 Miller Street, 41.731219, -71.286228

The Warren Boat Yard built minesweepers and coastal transports for the navy, with some being forwarded to the Soviet Union and Great Britain. See chapter 7, volume 1. The site is now occupied by Dyer Boats.

BRISTOL

Herreshoff Manufacturing Company, 1 Burnside Street, 41.663686, -71.273062

The famous Herreshoff Manufacturing Company constructed eight consecutive winning America's Cup sailing boats from 1893 to 1934 and the navy's first steam torpedo boat in 1877. At Herreshoff Shipyard on the Bristol waterfront, Herreshoff designed and built 100 small wooden-hulled vessels between October 1942 and 1945, including coastal transports, coastal minesweepers, PT boats and army/navy air-sea rescue boats. See chapter 7, volume 1.

A. Sidney DeWolf Herreshoff and Rebecca Chase Herreshoff converted the property into the Herreshoff Marine Museum in 1971. Today, the campus encompasses the large museum facility, the old family homestead, six former company buildings and a large portion of the company's waterfront. The museum displays some photographs of the World War II shipbuilding program.

EAST GREENWICH

Harris & Parsons Shipyard, 1 Division Street, 41.665739, -71.445847

The Harris & Parsons shipyard was just north of Division Street and the East Greenwich Yacht Club. It probably was where Prime Marina East Greenwich is today. The shipyard built eight submarine chasers and three other wooden vessels between 1943 and 1945. See chapter 7, volume 1.

NORTH KINGSTOWN

Camp Endicott (Naval Construction Training Center), 159 Allen Harbor Road, 41.619058, -71.410379

A Naval Construction Training Center, called Camp Endicott, was established at Davisville on June 27, 1942. The facility was expanded to cover a total of 1,892 acres. It was the home of the Naval Construction Battalions (Seabees). The first 296 men started training in February 1942. The center reached capacity in November 1942 when trainees totaled approximately 350 officers and 15,000 men. More than 100,000 of them trained at Davisville, along with 7,960 officers, many of whom attended Civil Engineer Corps Officer School. See chapter 4, volume 1 and chapter 14 in this book. The Davisville complex consisted of more than 200 buildings, mostly wood, constructed on the 250-acre site east of Davisville Road. Many remaining structures from the war were demolished in 1999 and 2000 in a state redevelopment program.

Surprisingly, a few of the massive warehouses used at Camp Endicott during the war still are used today. They include warehouses located at 123 Ocean Drive (off Davisville Road) currently used by Ocean State Oil; 192 Smith Street, currently used by Specialty Diving Service; 330 Romano Vineyard Way (off Mason Street) currently used by LJM Packaging; 370 Commerce Park Road currently used by Custom Design (on the other side of Romano Vineyard Way, opposite LJM Packaging); and 100 Tidal Drive currently used by North Atlantic Distribution Inc.

Seabees Museum and Memorial Park, 21 Iafrate Way, 41.606783, -71.449407

The Seabee Museum, on a small part of the western portion of Camp Endicott, documents the history of the Seabees. It has a variety of Quonset huts, pontoons (under the Seabee statue), regimental stone markers and other exhibits that can be viewed outside. While visitors can roam the grounds at any time, its small indoor museum has limited hours.

George A. Fuller Company, in 1941, designed the Quonset hut at Quonset Point. More than 32,000 were manufactured at Fuller's West Davisville factory and shipped overseas, before manufacturing operations were shifted to factories in the Midwest. See chapter 4, volume 1. A few

Some Seabee battalions established at Davisville had large markers carved and placed in front of their battalion offices. This one, for the 115th Construction Battalion, commissioned in February 1943, is displayed at the Seabee Museum and Memorial Park in Davisville. *Christian McBurney.*

World War II–era Quonset huts are scattered throughout the state, with the largest concentrations in North Kingstown at the Seabee Museum and in Shore Acres on Kingsley Avenue. At Allen Harbor, Quonset huts are used for storage at the North Kingstown Marina (off of Allen Harbor Road and Davisville Road), next door by the U.S. Food and Drug Administration and at the yacht club on the west side of Allen Harbor (off Sanford Road). One Quonset hut that reportedly stored ammunition during the war, called the Moore House, located at 4375 Main Road in Tiverton, currently can be rented for overnight stays.

Naval Air Station Quonset Point, 1584 Quonset Road, 41.597814, -71.412206

Quonset Point became the largest naval air facility in the Northeast. See chapter 3, volume 1, and appendix A. The construction project, including a massive dredging project, estimated to take two years, was completed in one, in July 1941. In addition to three runways, four land plane and two seaplane hangars (Buildings 1 and 2) were constructed, along with control towers, barracks for 1,680 men, underground storage for three million gallons of gasoline and an aircraft carrier pier 80 feet wide and 1,172 feet long. Some 11,000 civilian workers, men and women of all trades and professions, worked at the naval air station around the clock, seven days a week. A Naval Training School for reserve officers graduated hundreds of

"90-day wonders" every three months. The top graduates were offered to attend the nation's only Air Combat Intelligence School. Some British pilots also came here to learn to operate U.S. fighter aircraft supplied to Britain. The first night-fighter training for pilots occurred at Quonset until moved to Charlestown in 1943. Quonset Point also hosted other schools, including a gunnery school for aircrews and a celestial navigation school. Seaplanes flew from Quonset on missions to hunt for German submarines. The facility served an important naval aviation function after the war but closed in 1974. See chapter 3, volume 1, and chapter 11.

Most of Quonset's more than 500 World War II–era buildings have disappeared, but a few remain.

Buildings 1 and 2 (also called Hangars 1 and 2), the first large structures constructed at the naval air station, still exist, located at the waterside on MacNaught Street at the corner of John Thomas Street (which is off Roger Williams Way). They housed PBY and PBM seaplanes that searched for German U-boat activity in neutrality patrols starting in late 1939. Building 2 was completed in 1939 and Building 1 in 1941. Each is 240 feet long, 373 feet wide and 44 feet tall, with a floor space of 101,760 square feet. A seaplane control tower atop Building 2 disappeared shortly after the end of the war.

Quonset Point is now the home of a number of industrial and defense contracting businesses, primarily General Dynamics's Electric Boat division, the manufacturer of navy submarines. In about 1999, General Dynamics sold Buildings 1 and 2 to Senseco Marine, which continues to use these facilities in its business of building double-hulled barges and tugboats.

The core of the original Aviation Operations Building (Building 61), which contained the air traffic controllers, still exists at 150 Airport Street (at the corner of Dillabur Avenue). Completed in 1941, it also housed radar and radio communications equipment, and its telephone lines made it possible to communicate with army, navy and coast guard posts at Newport and Boston, as well as along the East Coast from Canada to the Florida Keys. This building may be slated for destruction, as a replacement air control tower was constructed a few years ago. Next to the core of the former Aviation Operations Building is the sole remaining runway of three. This site, now Quonset State Airport, is used by the Rhode Island Air National Guard, the Rhode Island Army National Guard and some private civilian aircraft.

Just up from the airport, on Dillabur Avenue on the right, is the site of the important Assembly & Repair Building (Building 60), where hundreds of

Link trainers were used to teach pilots how to rely on celestial navigation to fly their planes when they were over the ocean or otherwise far away from friendly radio signals. These pilots are operating the trainer at Quonset Point on March 4, 1944. Four towers that housed them survived into the 1990s, but they have since been demolished. *National Archives.*

aircraft designated for aircraft carriers were refurbished by the A&R Unit. Completed in 1941, it was the largest building at Quonset: 650 feet long, 632 feet wide and 59 feet high, with a floor space of 386,671 square feet. It suffered an explosion and fire in 1948, after which much of it was rebuilt. It still looks much like the original building. Now owned and used by Electric Boat, it is a top-secret facility.

At 112 Dillabur Avenue is former Building 16, the Navy Supply building, completed in 1941. The concrete three-to-four-story building is 343 feet long, 141 feet wide, 43 feet tall, with a floor space of 143,320 square feet. Next door is former Building 17, also completed in 1941, which was used to store aircraft parts. Both buildings are (or will be) used by Electric Boat.

The wharf off 1390 Roger Williams Way, now a Senseco Marine location, was the carrier pier used by aircraft carriers in World War II. It cannot be seen from the road. The dock, or Pier No. 1, at the end of Davisville Road, built in 1942, was used by the Advance Base Depot. It is a 1,200-foot-long-by-250-foot-wide timber pile-supported pier that during the war was used to ship materials and supplies to navy bases worldwide. It can be seen from Maritime Way. It is now in the Port of Davisville and is used for international cargo, including servicing massive automobile carriers.

Two facilities were built for, and frequently used by, officers based at Quonset during the war. The officers' club, then and today called the O Club, on Lt. James Brown Road, is now used for special functions. The golf course (then just nine holes) is open to the public as the North Kingstown Golf Course.

WICKFORD

Perkins & Vaughan, 125 Steamboat Avenue,
41.571466, -71.443923

Perkins & Vaughan, the wartime operator of the Vaughan Shipyard, is called the Wickford Shipyard today, although it operates only as a marina. It built nine 110-foot submarine chasers and three other small warships between 1942 and 1945. See chapter 7, volume 1.

DUTCH ISLAND

Fort Greble, 41.503249, -71.400810

Fort Greble was half a mile northeast of Fort Kearney and one mile west of Conanicut Island. It occupied almost the entire island, except for a six-acre portion on the south side occupied by the lighthouse. There are gun emplacements and ruins of fort buildings remaining. The island was used as a rifle range in the 1940s, but this use was discontinued in December 1947. Remaining gun platforms date from the Civil War era. A Word War I–era concrete freshwater cistern collapsed in 2000, forcing the island's closure to the public for several years. The island is now the Dutch Island State Wildlife Management Area and is mostly overgrown and not maintained. It is accessible only by private boat.

Saunderstown

Fort Kearney, 166 Ferry Road, 41.490556, -71.422778

Fort Kearney was near the South Ferry Landing opposite Conanicut Island. The fort protected the West Passage of Narragansett Bay. See chapter 10, volume 1. The site is now part of the campus of the University of Rhode Island's Graduate School of Oceanography. Plenty of parking is available.

Battery French and Battery Cram were located between Aquarium Road. and Fish Road. Gun emplacements for two 3-inch barbette guns of Battery Armistead and two 6-inch disappearing rifles of Battery Cram (on Bunker Road) still exist. The latter may be the largest surviving gun emplacements in the state. A small research atomic reactor was built on top of Battery French in 1963–64. The concrete structures for Battery Cram and Battery Armistead still stand but are not occupied. The fire-control post, used to identify enemy vessels and direct artillery fire against them, is still located to the right of the south entrance from South Ferry Road. The concrete slab with three steel rings built into it that anchored the antisubmarine cable across the West Passage is on the rocky beach about thirty yards south of the wharf.

The fort was used as a unique prisoner-of-war camp in 1945, holding POWs opposed to the Nazi regime. It was the headquarters of a program to reeducate German prisoners with democratic values, one element of which was the publication of the German-language newspaper *Der Ruf* (*The Call*) for distribution at POW camps across the country. See chapter 11, volume 1.

South Kingstown

Hannah Robinson Tower, MacSparran Hill, 41.495585, -71.455980

The wooden Observation Tower, a well-known landmark at the intersection of U.S. Route 1 and Route 138 at MacSparran Hill, was built by the Rhode Island Department of Public Works and completed in 1938. During the war it was used by the United States Army Signal Corps, which enclosed the sides for protection against bad weather and maintained a 24-hour watch. It was returned to the state after the war. The tower was rebuilt using the same pillars in 1988. During the war a viewer could see below a broad valley and Newport, but today tall trees obscure the view.

Shaun McBurney stands in front of a gun emplacement on Bunker Road at former Fort Kearney. It is one of the largest surviving gun emplacements in the state. *Christian McBurney.*

The antisubmarine net that crossed the West Passage from Fort Getty was anchored to this concrete slab on the beach in front of Fort Kearney (now the home of the Narragansett Bay Campus of the University of Rhode Island). Neil Ross sits on the slab, giving perspective to its size. *Brooks William Ross.*

NARRAGANSETT

Fort Varnum, 98 Cormorant Road, 41.446005, -71.435278

Fort Varnum (now called Camp James M. Varnum or Camp Varnum) is off Boston Neck Road in the area of Cormorant Road near Whale Rock Point Road. Batteries here were New Battery House (6-inch guns), New Battery Armistead (3-inch guns) and Anti Motor Torpedo Boat Battery 921 (90-millimeter carriage guns), near the shore. The fort overlooks Whale Rock and the bay south of Beavertail Point. The site had a dual searchlight with on-site radar support and several concrete fire-control stations disguised as typical New England beach houses. Four still remain. These points transmitted aiming data to batteries at Fort Greene, Fort Church and Fort Wetherill.

Camp Varnum has the best collection of remaining World War II–era structures in the state. The multicolored buildings were designed to look like, in the aggregate, an oceanside village (see cover of book for aerial view).

Two 90mm gun batteries, with a fire control building in rear, at Fort Varnum, March 1944. The building and gun platforms survive today. *Rhode Island Army National Guard.*

One of the four remaining fire-control buildings has a room overlooking the bay with color stenciling on its walls showing flags that correspond with letters of the alphabet, for communicating with friendly ships offshore in case radio and other communications systems broke down, as well as a sign for the battalion stationed there (see the three images at the top on the book's back cover). The two main batteries, each camouflaged under a grassy hill, still exist, as do most of their cement interior rooms. Circular gun blocks for the 90-millimeter guns and two 6-inch steel-shielded guns on barbette carriages are still clearly visible near the outer fence.

Camp Varnum today is used (and preserved) by the Rhode Island National Guard. Public access is restricted, but visitors can take a trail around the fence line to see most of the former fort. Traveling south on Boston Neck Road (Route 1A), take a left onto Old Boston Neck Road. Go one-quarter of a mile and come to a large "No Trespassing" sign. Immediately to the left is a dirt road and small parking lot, and the start of a Nature Conservancy trail called Whale Rock Preserve. Walking east about fifteen minutes, much of it on wooden planks, walkers come to the fence line. (This stretch can be very muddy in places in soggy conditions.) Walking along the fence line will take you to the front of Camp Varnum and the rocky beach. Views of existing World War II sites at Camp Varnum, and the closest view from land of Whale Rock, can be seen. The Narragansett Historical Society occasionally gives tours of World War II sites and includes this stroll.

Bonnet Point, 274 Colonel John Gardner Road, 41.472158, -71.418765

Control stations for mines, consisting of a manhole and searchlights, were located at Bonnet Point. One station remains in the backyard (bayside) of a private residence at 274 Colonel John Gardner Road.

Kinney Bungalow, 505 Point Judith Road, 41.407280, -71.478931

Built by Francis Kinney in 1899 as a private clubhouse for post–polo game parties, it was used during the war as a communications post for Fort Greene.

Fort Greene (Fishermen's State Memorial Park,
1011 Point Judith Road, 41.3812135, -71.4895008;
Fort Nathanael Greene United States Army Reserve Center,
970 Point Judith Road, 41.381485, -71.487267;
Point Judith Fishermen's Memorial, 1399 Memorial Drive,
41.430988, -71.456791)

During the war, Fort Greene was divided into three separate parcels, called "reservations." The West Reservation, which included Battery 109, is now Fishermen's Memorial State Park, along with most of the former southern parcel. Battery 109 included a massive concrete gun emplacement, mostly hidden under an artificially made hill camouflaged with grass, designed to house two 16-inch guns at each end. It exists today. The opening for one gun is just 100 yards west–southwest of the park office *(41.379921, -71.490875)* at 1011 Point Judith Road. Part of the cement structure for the battery can be seen protruding from the south side of the hill. A path leads to the top of the hill, where a gun emplacement or lookout support still exists. Inside the casemate (the hill), which is off-limits to visitors, is a concrete corridor about 500 feet long connecting this casement with another one intended to hold the other 16-inch gun. Off this corridor and in between the two gun emplacements are concrete rooms to store shells for each gun, and in the middle a room that housed power generating facilities. The massive guns were brought to the site but never installed. To the west within the park is an earth-covered bunker that formerly held a plotting room to support the battery; its interior is sealed off.

Nearby to the northeast, a concrete fire-control tower still stands, one of the few remaining in existence, adjacent to the park office and parking lot. It is disguised as a farm silo. It was used to observe, identify and pinpoint enemy vessels and positions and to relay information about the accuracy of artillery fire. The wide opening (window) was for viewing with a large optical rangefinder, which is like a periscope mounted horizontally on a pedestal. The observer looked through the eyepiece in the center of the horizontal viewer (transit). The line of sight was transferred to each end of the transit, and the observer focused on the target. This triangulated the target's position, providing the range of fire for the artillery.

The gambrel-roofed barn and other supporting structures next to the fire-control tower and behind the office date from the war. The buildings, originally designed to appear like a farm complex, have been significantly

Part of the concrete remains of the bunker, disguised as a hill, designed to hold one of the 16-inch guns at Fort Greene, is now part of Fishermen's Memorial State Park. The overhang extends over what would have been the gun port opening. *Christian McBurney.*

modified. The "barn" was used as an ordnance repair shop and the one-story shop for motor repair. Only campers using the facilities are allowed in the park, but from November to early April, visitors might be allowed in. The Narragansett Historical Society tour also includes this site.

The East Reservation included Battery Hamilton (or Battery 108). It contained the same type of underground concrete structure as at Fishermen's Memorial, except in this battery the two massive 16-inch guns were actually installed. Shells fired from these guns weighed over a ton each and could reach a distance of 26 miles. Some 32 rounds were fired from the guns for test purposes (shattering windows for two or three miles around, according to a local resident). The battery fired, for example, 3 rounds on August 6, 1943. Today, the former 105-acre East Reservation is called the Fort Nathanael Greene United States Army Reserve Center. The fenced-off site, on the east side of Point Judith Drive approaching Fishermen's Memorial State Park, is closed to the public. Authorized visitors to the base report that the concrete structures are still in place and in good condition and that the gun

This cylindrical fire-control tower at former Fort Greene (now part of Fishermen's Memorial State Park) is disguised as a farm silo. *Norman Desmarais.*

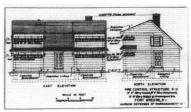

The left image shows two two-story fire control structures that were part of the South Reservation at Fort Greene in Narragansett on Narragansett Bay. During the war, the two structures were enclosed in a wooden façade designed to appear like a summer cottage (see army plans on the right). The stone steps to the wooden structure are still visible. *Christopher Zeeman (right) and National Archives (left).*

openings remain open. An aerial view reveals the artificial hills that housed former Battery 108 and its supporting plotting room bunker. The stone gate at the reserve's entrance may also date to the war. Authorized visitors do not believe there are any other World War II remains at the base.

The South Reservation, off 1414 Ocean Road and near the Point Judith Fishermen's Memorial at 1399 Memorial Drive (part of Fishermen's Memorial State Park), included Battery 211 and was at the water's edge. Battery 211 had two 6-inch steel-shielded guns on barbette carriages. A concrete circular gun emplacement for one of the 6-inch guns is at the shoreline. A three-level, earth-covered fire-control bunker still remains (*41.364088, -71.486648*) but is now in disrepair. The top of the bunker has nice views.

Three fire-control stations disguised to resemble typical beach houses were once located close by. Standing on top of the mound covering the bunker discussed immediately above and viewing north, one of the concrete structures can be seen in front of a residential neighborhood. The concrete remains of one of them is across the street from 1014 Ocean Drive. They consist of two concrete two-story fire-control structures that during the war had a wooden façade built around them. The site can be accessed by turning into 1000 Ocean Drive and taking a left, but the area is a new development that is private property with a sign warning against trespassing. In winter, the two structures can be seen from Ocean Drive.

CHARLESTOWN

Naval Auxiliary Air Facility Charlestown, 5 Park Lane, 41.372326, -71.664356

Naval Auxiliary Air Facility Charlestown was largely built in 1942, with berthing for 700 personnel, but it expanded to house more than 1,600 and construction continued to war's end. It started out training aircraft carrier pilots and had a catapult to simulate launchings on one of its three runways of 5,800, 5,470 and 4,800 feet. Future president George H.W. Bush served here from November 30, 1943, to mid-January 1944 (see chapter 7). In 1944 and 1945, it became the country's primary site for night-fighter training (see chapter 13, and chapter 3, volume 1). After the war, it became an air station and then a landing field, before closing in 1974.

Today, the former airfield, located southeast of the junction of US Route 1A (Old Post Road) and State Route 1 (Post Road), is used partially as a

This propeller is now a memorial at Ninigret Park, the former NAAF Charlestown, to Lieutenant Kenneth Bruce McQuady, who was killed when his F6F-5N Hellcat crashed on takeoff, its engine cutting out and his aircraft landing on the ice on Ninigret Pond on March 2, 1945. *Christian McBurney.*

town of Charlestown recreational park and the rest is Ninigret National Wildlife Refuge. Before the site opened to the public, practice bombs and contaminated soil were removed, and the few remaining structures demolished. A memorial (on Park Lane east of the tennis courts) erected in 1974 at the former airfield bears the names of the fifty-four pilots killed there in training accidents from 1943 through 1945 and seven others between 1947 and 1965. A nearby memorial contains the propeller from the F6F-5N Hellcat flown by Lieutenant Kenneth B. McQuady in a fatal night flight on March 2, 1945, in which his plane crashed at the end of the runway at Charlestown.

Currently, the northern half of the airfield is used for recreation, fairs and festivals. The southern portion of the runways has been covered with earth and gravel and is now part of the 900-acre Ninigret National Wildlife Refuge. The locations of the three runways can still be easily viewed.

Charlestown Historical Society, 4417B Old Post Road, 41.382966, -71.641583

The Charlestown Historical Society has an exhibit of photographs of Charlestown's Naval Auxiliary Air Facility during World War II, including several of George H.W. Bush. It also has a bomber jacket worn by a pilot who trained at Charlestown during the war, and a simulated standing bomb used in World War II photographs of officers who trained at Charlestown, with the inscription, "Thru These Portals Pass the Hottest Test Pilots in the World." Next to the Cross' Mills Public Library, it has limited visiting hours.

Quonochontaug Neck, 468 East Beach Road, 41.342358, -71.694674

A fire-control station consisting of cottages was set up at Quonochontaug Neck in Charlestown. One remains with a protected switchboard bunker at 468 East Beach Road near Blue Shutters Beach. This was primarily a communications bunker linked by cable to both the lookout station on Route 1 (see 5075 Post Road below) and the communications center on Block Island. Some residents report that the guns and ammunition used for target practice on the beach were stored here, but this has not been substantiated. Target practice was regularly held on East Beach, and people were not allowed to walk there. The "off limit" area stretched from Blue Shutters all the way to the Charlestown Breachway. See chapter 8.

A lookout station constructed behind the First Baptist Church of Charlestown at Quonochontaug (5075 Post Road, *41.357600, -71.703317*) housed eighteen men and a mess hall. It was made to look like a normal residence, and with its hilltop location, activity in Block Island Sound could be viewed. Communication cables linked this station with the bunker on East Beach Road. Another fire-control station, consisting of a tower and searchlights, was located at Ninigret (*41.354246, -71.651417*), now part of the Ninigret National Wildlife Refuge. Some married officers and their wives were housed at the nearby Wilcox Tavern (5153 Old Post Road). The Quonochontaug Historical Society has some photographs of World War II sites in the area (visit by appointment only).

An army base camp with infantry and artillery units was located at what is now Burlingame State Park north of Quonochontaug (75 Burlingame State Park Road 41.373026, -71.693202). The infantry of B Company of the 181st Infantry Regiment patrolled the coast between Jerusalem and Watch Hill. Apparently, nothing remains of Camp Burlingame from the wartime era.

WESTERLY

Naval Auxiliary Air Facility Westerly, 52 Airport Road, 41.349697, -71.802922

Naval Auxiliary Air Facility Westerly was bounded by Airport Road and Franklin Street (US Route 1). The civilian airport's runways were expanded, and it was commissioned on June 1, 1943, as an auxiliary to Quonset Point. Initially hosting torpedo squadrons, in 1944 and 1945 it specialized in night-fighter training. In March 1944, it hosted 104 officers and 719 men. At least 4 pilots are known to have been killed from crashes of their planes flying from this airport (for a rescue from a failed landing see chapter 6).

The site is now Westerly State Airport and is known for its flights to Block Island. The control tower/passenger terminal building burned down in 1998. The only wartime remains are a utility building used to house vehicles and the runways (which were narrowed after the war).

EXETER

Rhode Island Veterans Memorial Cemetery,
301 South County Trail (Route 2), 41.544920, -71.536224

Rhode Island veterans who meet certain qualifications can be buried at no cost with military honors. The dignified and solemn military cemetery on 280 acres is maintained by the Rhode Island Office of Veterans Affairs and includes 31 monuments dedicated to veterans of wars and conflicts.

CONANICUT ISLAND (JAMESTOWN)

Fort Getty, 1050 Fort Getty Road, 41.491471, -71.399024

A detachment of Coast Artillery from Fort Adams, including personnel of Batteries A and B, was quartered in the new barracks at Fort Getty in late 1940. Battery A was assigned to the 6-inch guns of Battery House and Battery B to the 3-inch guns of Battery Whiting, a smaller emplacement at the entrance to the reservation. For more on its wartime operations, see chapter 12. Toward the end of the war, the fort was used as a unique prisoner-of-war camp for German anti-Nazis. See chapter 12, volume 1.

The fortifications were demolished after the war and buried with landfill, but there is still a Battery Whiting gun emplacement (*41.487841, -71.397887*) to the left of the park entrance, a fire-control bunker near the shore in the southwest corner, and beyond this bunker a concrete block used to anchor the antisubmarine nets across the West Passage to Fort Kearney. A row of similar blocks exist as mooring tethers adjacent to a boat ramp. The stone gate entrance was constructed by POWs in 1945. The site became a Town of Jamestown park in 1955 and is used as a summer campground.

Prospect Hill, 43 Battery Lane, 41.480662, -71.393179

Battery Lane is about a third of a mile south of the junction of Fort Getty Road and Beavertail Road. The road is named for the Conanicut Battery, a Revolutionary War–era fortification that was manned at various times by colonial, British and French troops. A small parking lot is located at the end of Battery Lane. An interpretive sign at the edge gives an orientation to the site. The path on the right goes to the Conanicut Battery. The one on the left goes up Prospect Hill to six sunken concrete bunkers that were used as observation posts and for fire control during World War II. Although Prospect Hill's elevation is only 132 feet, it is the highest point on this part of Conanicut Island. During the war, there were no trees in this area, providing a clear view of the bay. Today, the hill is covered with vegetation, but the bunkers are still clearly visible.

The site served the harbor mining effort as a communications link for the operations of Commands 1 and 2 in the East and West Passages of Narragansett Bay. The Mine Command operated a 172-foot army mine planter, several 64-foot craft and a group of mine yawls docked at Forts Wetherill and Adams. Fire-control points for the mine fields later established were constructed on Beavertail Point between Hull Cove (*41.464444, -71.388598*) and Austin Hollow (*41.465977, -71.396517*). The army established permanent roadblocks along the road in this area in 1942 to curtail traffic to Fort Burnside and Beavertail Lighthouse, less than one mile farther south. See chapter 12.

The Hull Cove mine casemate was just west of Beavertail Road on what is now private property. The casemate now serves as the basement of a private residence. Two inverted torpedoes embedded in the driveway's gate identify the property. On the east side of Beavertail Road is a small parking lot, from which a path leads to Hull Cove and the cable hut that fed the East Passage minefields; the site includes remnants of the cables and connections.

Spraycliff Observatory, 585 Beavertail Road, 41.461910, -71.397429

The Spraycliff Observatory was a top-secret facility for developing and testing airborne radar systems. See chapter 13. It was located on the west side of Beavertail Road. The observatory's operations were deactivated in 1946, and the area became a transmitter site as part of Naval Radio Station Newport. Closed in 1974, the site is now part of Beavertail State Park. The laboratories, equipment, administrative buildings and antennae at former Spraycliff Observatory have all been dismantled, moved or destroyed. The site is now overgrown with vegetation. What little remains of it includes a large antenna tuning hut, some deteriorated asphalt roads and a concrete water cistern.

Harbor Entrance Command Post, 800 Beavertail Road
41.454718, -71.397185

The army and navy jointly managed the Harbor Entrance Command Post (HECP) for Narragansett Bay, which managed all vessel traffic entering or leaving the bay plus supervised the antisubmarine nets on both the East and West Passages. See chapter 12. The observation and command station became operational in July 1943. After the war, the building was used as a navy transmitter site until 1974. The property is now part of Beavertail State Park. Some non-operating radio and radar towers installed in the postwar years are still on the grounds. The still-impressive building is currently rented to a live-in custodian and is treated as a private residence.

Beavertail Lighthouse Museum, 736 Beavertail Road,
41.449447, -71.399450

During the war, the coast guard operated the lighthouse on the southernmost point of Conanicut Island and a searchlight located in front of the lighthouse on the foundation of the original lighthouse. Boatswain's Mate Joe Burbine had the merchant vessel *Black Point* in view when it was torpedoed by *U-853* (see chapter 13, volume 1). He immediately telephoned the news to his commanding officer's office, which then notified the Coast Guard Section Base in Newport by teletype. The base notified the navy, which sent out the news by radio to all stations.

Situated on property managed by the coast guard, the lighthouse remains an active navigation aid and now hosts the wonderful Beavertail Lighthouse Museum, run by a nonprofit organization. It includes a lighthouse, an exhibit on the Fresnel lens and electronic touchscreen tables and storyboards. The museum covers such topics as shipwrecks, hurricanes, lighthouses and the Beavertail Lighthouse itself, as well as Beavertail's role in World War II. It is open to the public with free admission during the summer.

Fort Burnside, 800 Beavertail Road, 41.453471, -71.397571

Battery Whiting (*41.451625, -71.397246*) was relocated from Fort Getty to Fort Burnside, situated behind (north of) the Beavertail Lighthouse during the summer of 1942. See chapter 12. Its guns covered the East (main)

Entrance to ammunition bunker for two 3-inch artillery pieces at Battery Whiting, now in Beavertail State Park. *Varoujan Karentz.*

Passage, facing Brenton Point. Battery Whiting's weapons were emplaced on concrete gun blocks 100 feet apart and were partially protected by a circular embankment of earth thrown up around each. Partial remains still exist. To the rear and in the center of these positions, a small magazine and a battery command facility were constructed of concrete and covered with earth. This structure, which still exists, had only one entrance, facing west, away from the guns.

Fort Wetherill, 3 Fort Wetherill Road, 41.477799, -71.358515

Fort Wetherill was located on the southeastern shore of Conanicut Island, roughly two miles across the East Passage from Newport. Modern fortifications were first built here in 1899 and were expanded in World War I. During World War II, the fort was situated atop three 50-to-70-foot-high granite outcroppings and commanded an unobstructed view of the open sea to the south. It consisted of twelve batteries along a 300-foot front. Part of the 243rd Coast Artillery Regiment was transferred here from Fort Adams for training at four of the seven Endicott batteries from

View of part of the concrete remains of Fort Wetherill, much of which is now covered in graffiti. *Norman Desmarais.*

October to December 1940. Barracks were built to house the regiment's 1,200 soldiers. Antisubmarine nets went across the East Passage to Fort Adams. See chapter 12. As the threat of invasion subsided, in 1945 the site was converted to a special German POW camp. See chapter 12, volume 1.

Much of the cement fort structure and gun emplacements remain, although the walls are covered with graffiti and many of the steps are crumbling. The surrounding area became a state park in 1972. At Bull Point, the waterfront mine, munitions and cable storage buildings were occupied by the Jamestown Public Works Department. In 2003, the state's Department of Environmental Management's Marine Fisheries Section refurbished the buildings as its headquarters. Two buildings have train tracks running into them: one of them was a mine storage building (now used for vehicle storage and repair by the Jamestown Highway Department and in a dilapidated condition) and the other was a former mine cable storage building.

USO Recreation Center, 41 Conanicus Avenue, 41.495767, -71.367753

Over the town's strenuous objection, in 1942 the USO (United Service Organization) built an entertainment and recreation center for servicemen stationed in Jamestown on the site where the Gardner House Hotel once stood. The town purchased the building in 1946. It is now the Jamestown Recreation Center.

AQUIDNECK ISLAND PORTSMOUTH

Motor Torpedo Boat Squadrons Training Center, Naval Net Depot, and Naval Supply Depot, between King Charles Drive and Stringham Road, west of West Main Road (RI-114), 41.586900, -71.280433

The Motor Torpedo Boat Squadrons Training Center was located in the Melville section of Portsmouth on Aquidneck Island. This location was the nation's main training facility for training sailors to use PT (patrol torpedo) boats; squadrons of PT boats also patrolled Narragansett Bay and the Rhode Island coast. A separate unit repaired PT boats. See chapter 5, volume 1. The Training Center trained 2,017 officers and 17,500 enlisted men, including Ensign John F. Kennedy, who afterward commanded a PT boat patrolling Rhode Island's waters (see chapter 4). With war's end, the training school and remaining PT boat squadrons were quickly decommissioned. Nothing remains of its former glory.

PT Boats Inc., a nonprofit organization, placed a bronze marker at the foot of the flagpole (*41.590295, -71.283156*) in front of the marina office of New England Boatworks on Lagoon Avenue in 1976 to honor PT boaters killed in action during the war. It is flanked by a 40-millimeter gun and a torpedo.

Melville also hosted the Naval Fuel Depot (located on the north side of Stringham Road) and the Naval Net Depot, the first of its kind in the United States, but nothing remains of them.

Prudence Island, 41.585292, -71.332903,
and Hope Island, 41.602051, -71.366972

Both Prudence Island and Hope Island were used for weapons storage facilities. The southern tip of Prudence Island, part of the town of Portsmouth, was purchased as a site of a naval magazine for the storage of ammunition in April 1942. In addition to the 25 magazines built there in 1942, facilities were built to support assigned personnel. Housing consisted of barracks for 224 men, married and bachelor officer quarters, a mess hall and a recreation building. A 50,000-gallon concrete reservoir was placed underground for fresh water. A 500-foot T-shaped pier was built extending to the south to facilitate loading and offloading. The site was placed under the control of the Torpedo Station (on Goat Island) on July 8, 1944. The site is now part of South Prudence Bay Island Park. Bunkers for storing ammunition were built throughout Hope Island in 1940 and 1941, in support of NAS Quonset Point.

Middletown

Sachuest Point, end of Sachuest Point Road, Middletown,
41.473165, -71.247093

A Naval Rifle Range, with eight ranges, barracks for 700 men and other support buildings, was located on 165 acres at Sachuest Point. Also located here were radar, searchlights, fire-control stations disguised as cottages and a lookout tower designed as a silo. Later, the receiver site for the Naval Communication Station Newport was established here. The site is now the Sachuest Point National Wildlife Refuge. Some concrete remains still exist. Two old 4.72-inch guns were also redeployed from Boston Harbor to here during the war; one of the guns is reportedly now on display at Ansonia, Connecticut.

Newport

Naval Training Station 1378 Porter Avenue
41.509898, -71.326708

Naval Operating Base, Chandler Street, 41.522222, -71.308889

The Naval Training Station at Newport (NTS Newport), the navy's first onshore recruit training facility, was established on Coasters Harbor Island in 1883. During World War II, numerous facilities were constructed to support it at Coddington Point (none of which survive).

After Pearl Harbor, 8,600 recruits per month were in training by NTS Newport. A total of 204,115 recruits received training at the NTS Newport between 1939 and 1944. From 1943 through 1946, another 300,000 sailors underwent pre-commissioning ship training. The navy's housing and other support facilities expanded significantly on Aquidneck Island. After the war, some of the housing for enlisted men and Torpedo Station workers at Tonomy Hill was converted into low-income housing. See chapter 6, volume 1.

On April 2, 1941, Naval Operating Base Newport (NOB Newport) was founded on Coasters Harbor Island. Its commander coordinated all navy functions in Narragansett Bay and surrounding areas, including at Fall River and New Bedford, Massachusetts. Its facilities extended into Middletown. See chapter 6, volume 1.

During the war, NTS Newport was the headquarters of the navy's Atlantic Fleet, with the cruiser USS *Augusta* or three-masted ship USS *Constellation* used as the flagship. See chapters 1 and 2. Moorings in the bay saw heavy cruisers, destroyers, supply ships and net minding ships, as well as small "escort" aircraft carriers.

Naval Station Newport is currently home port for several ships from the coast guard and the National Oceanic and Atmospheric Administration. It occasionally maintains inactive navy vessels at its pier facilities as well. In the 2005 Base Realignment and Closure, the station gained over 500 billets and received, again, the Officer Candidate School (OCS), the Naval Supply Corps School (in 2011) and several other activities.

Luce Hall, Building 1, Luce Avenue, 41.507483, -71.329520, and Other Naval War College Buildings

The Naval War College (NWC), located on Coasters Harbor Island, reduced its operations during the war, but prior to it performed crucial war planning studies for the naval war in the Pacific (including for the "island hopping" strategy that was adopted). Admirals Ernest King, Raymond Spruance and Chester Nimitz were prewar NWC graduates. See chapter 6, volume 1. Luce Hall, built in 1892, the NWC's main administration building, also served as headquarters of NOB Newport. NOB Newport's first commander, and also the NWC's president, Admiral Edward C. Kalbfus, flew his admiral's flag atop Luce Hall. It was here that King and Kalbfus learned of the Pearl Harbor attack details on December 7, 1941. Sims Hall (29 Cushing Road *41.510907, -71.328392*), built in 1904, was used as a barrack (Barrack C) for trainees who came through NTS Newport. Today, it is used as overflow office space. Other NWC buildings existing at the time of the war and still standing are Mahan Hall (1904, at the rear of Luce Hall) and Pringle Hall (1934, to the west of Luce Hall). As part of the buildup in defenses to protect Newport, a 5-inch antiaircraft gun battery was installed on the top of the hill where the parking lot for McCarty Little Hall is now located. No buildings constructed on Coasters Harbor Island during the war currently exist.

Naval War College Museum, Founders Hall, 686 Cushing Road, 41.507455, -71.328199

The outstanding Naval War College Museum is located on Coasters Harbor Island at historic Founders Hall. Its exhibits focus on the history of: 1) the Naval War College since 1884; 2) naval activities in Narragansett Bay since the colonial period; and 3) the art and science of naval warfare since ancient times. It often has World War II exhibits. The two propellers of the German U-boat sunk off Point Judith in May 1945 (see chapter 13, volume 1, including a photo of them) are on display outside the museum. A special advance pass is needed to visit the museum, but it is worth the small effort. During the war, Founders Hall was effectively the headquarters of NTS Newport.

Newport Naval Hospital, 992 3rd Street, 41.501392, -71.320556

The staff of the Newport Naval Hospital complex during the war included about 95 male Navy doctors, 117 female nurses in the Navy Nurse Corps and hundreds more women and men serving as technicians, nursing assistants and in other posts. The hospital complex cared for thousands of sick NTS trainees and had 1,400 patients at one time. A German submariner who survived the sinking of *U-550* off Nantucket in April 1944 was brought to the hospital but died three weeks later of his injuries (see chapter 13, volume 1). The main hospital building, constructed in 1909, has been closed for almost three decades and may be acquired by the City of Newport.

Island Cemetery Annex, 30 Warner Street, 41.495810, -71.313431

Many famous Newporters are buried in this private cemetery, including Oliver Hazard Perry and Matthew Calbraith Perry. Tucked away in a corner of Island Cemetery in Newport is a section containing the graves of eight British and Commonwealth officers and enlisted men who died in training accidents while in the United States in 1943 and one in 1944 (see chapter 3, volume 1). The Royal Navy graves are located on Evarts Street along the fence line in a small section of the Island Cemetery at the corner of Brandt Street and Van Zandt Avenue, Navy Section Plots 172–177, graves 12–20.

Two German submariners are buried here, including the temporary survivor of *U-550*. In the summer of 1960, a scuba diver removed the remains of a crewman from *U-853*, which were buried with full military honors at the cemetery. See chapter 13, volume 1.

Government Landing, 53 America's Cup Avenue, 41.488909, -71.316868

The Jamestown Ferry and the ferry to the Naval Torpedo Station on Goat Island were located here. Sailors boarded launches to go to their warships, mostly destroyers, anchored in the harbor. The site included a parade ground for rallies, military exercise and Memorial Day services during the war.

Perrotti Park, the Newport City Harbor Master's Office and the Newport Harbor Hotel and Marina occupy part of the original site today.

Newport Armory, 365 Thames Street, 41.483211, -71.315124

The Newport Armory's 6,000 square feet was used as a training center for the first trainees from the Motor Torpedo Boat Squadrons Training Center in Melville. The facility ceased operation in the 1980s. The building was recently sold and will become the National Sailing Hall of Fame.

Newport Casino, 186-202 Bellevue Avenue, 41.482631, -71.308268

During the war, the navy rented the second floor of the Newport Casino for an officers' club. Ping-pong tables, a jukebox and a reading room were available. A good meal could be purchased for $1.25. Four outstanding grass tennis courts could be used, and an officers' tennis tournament started in 1944.

USO Locations

According to the Newport Historical Society, Newport had six USO (United Service Organizations) entertainment and recreation clubs, including the United Baptist Church, at 30 Spring Street, and the Edward Street Clubhouse, built in 1944, now the Martin Luther King Center. The Edward Street Clubhouse, located at 20 Marcus Wheatland Boulevard, served as a USO club for black and other servicemen of color. White servicemen were hosted at the USO club on Commercial Wharf, south of America's Cup Avenue, then one of the country's largest.

Fort Adams, 90 Fort Adams Drive, 41.478946, -71.337773

A harbor defense control post and an antiaircraft battery were located at impressive Fort Adams, as were several mobile 90-millimeter guns. The antisubmarine nets that stretched across the East Passage to Fort Wetherill were controlled from Fort Adams. See chapter 12. The former commandant's quarters was used by President Dwight D. Eisenhower as a summer White House in 1958 and 1960 and is now known as the Eisenhower House. The post was transferred to the navy in 1949 and became a state park in 1965. Well preserved, it is open to the public with guided tours and has a small maritime museum.

Brenton Point Military Reservation, 481 Ocean Avenue, 41.450392, -71.355044

The Brenton Point Military Reservation was located in what is now Brenton Point State Park between 1941 and 1946. It consisted of an unnamed battery of four 155-millimeter guns on Panama mounts, Anti-Motor Torpedo Boat Battery No. 923 and two radar towers and searchlights. Three Panama mounts were removed in 1989, but one remains southeast of the park building and west of the end of Atlantic Avenue, near a parking lot.

Naval Anti-Aircraft Training Center, Price's Neck Road, 41.450374, -71.337166

A Naval Anti-Aircraft Training Center for 20-millimeter, 40-millimeter and 3-inch antiaircraft guns was located on Price's Neck, along the southern shore of the city. The center consisted of 89 buildings, constructed on over 26 acres, and 29 antiaircraft guns. There was even a tilting platform to simulate the pitch and roll that would be experienced onboard a ship. Concrete remnants of the firing line still remain.

Antiaircraft Battery, 86 Bliss Road 41.499860, -71.300550

Four 5-inch naval antiaircraft guns, later replaced by four 90-millimeter antiaircraft guns, were located at the intersection of Eustis Avenue and Bliss Road. The gate to the military compound was at Loyola Terrace. These sites had reinforced-concrete emplacements, steel igloo-style surface magazines, underground concrete ammunition magazines and housing, mess and sanitation facilities. While most of the gun supports are gone, a few houses were built on parts of them as supports, including at 19 Xavier Terrace. Ruggles Avenue had a similar battery, but none of it remains.

Aerial view of the antiaircraft battery on Bliss Road in Newport, 1943. Only a few remnants remain today. A similar battery was located on Ruggles Avenue near what is now William S. Rodgers High School. *Naval War College Museum.*

GOAT ISLAND

Naval Torpedo Station, 2 Goat Island Road, 41.487661, -71.327679

The Naval Torpedo Station produced many of the navy's torpedoes in both World War I and World War II. It became the largest single industrial employer in the state early in the war, with more than 12,600 employees, many of them women. The facility on Goat Island operated twenty-four hours a day, seven days a week, producing approximately one-third of the 57,653 torpedoes manufactured for the navy between January 1, 1939, and June 1, 1946. See chapter 2, volume 1. There were also twelve 20-millimeter antiaircraft guns and eighteen antiaircraft searchlight positions located at the Naval Torpedo Station.

The only former navy building remaining on the island is now the Goat Island Marina and Marina Bar & Grille. Hotels and condominiums now dominate the part of the island where the factory was located.

ROSE ISLAND

Rose Island (*41.496550, -71.342483*) served as a naval magazine during the war; most of the magazines were built in the 1890s and during World War I. The army operated antiaircraft batteries emplaced near the lighthouse. The four 5-inch naval guns were replaced by four 90-millimeter guns. Ruins of the antiaircraft batteries, fortifications and storage facilities can still be seen around the island. The lighthouse is now privately owned and can be rented by the week or the weekend. The Jamestown Newport Ferry stops at the island in the summer.

GOULD ISLAND

Gould Island, located in the East Passage north of Newport (*41.615312, -71.219722*), played in important role in the war despite its small size (56 acres). A seaplane hangar was located at the south end of the island and a torpedo testing facility at the north end. A degaussing station (a demagnetizing facility capable of neutralizing ships to prevent them from attracting or detonating magnetic mines or torpedoes) was put into operation on the island toward the end of 1942.

The large brick building that served as the overhaul shop and the long passage to the firing pier on the north end of the island dominated the island. Its remains can be seen today looking north from the Newport (Pell) Bridge. The torpedo range ran to the north approximately six miles, passing between Prudence Island and Hope Island. The facility was completed in 1943 and designed for proof-firing 100 torpedoes per day. It test-fired about 75,000 torpedoes during the war. The island was mostly deforested during the war, but today it is covered with trees. It reverted to the State of Rhode Island after 1975.

TIVERTON

Anti-Motor Torpedo Boat Battery, 1837 Main Road, 41.625375, -71.213744

A 40-millimeter Anti-Motor Torpedo Boat battery was located at the Stone Bridge in Tiverton. It was west of Fort Barton, near Grinnell's Beach and west of the intersection of SR 77 (Main Road) and Stone Bridge Road. There are no apparent remains.

LITTLE COMPTON

Fort Church Military Reservation

North or West Reservation (Battery Gray), 685 West Main Road, 41.479743, -71.182732

East Reservation (Battery Reilly), 16 Warren's Point Road, 41.473191, -71.171391

South Reservation (Battery 212), 43 Washington Road, 41.459900, -71.190217

The War Department established a military reservation at Sakonnet Point at West Main Road (SR 77) in Little Compton on December 11, 1941. It became known as Fort Church Military Reservation in honor of Colonel Benjamin Church, a famous fighter during King Philip's War from Little Compton. The complex consisted of three separate parcels: 1) North or West Reservation, called Battery Gray (present-day Sakonnet Golf Club); 2) East Reservation, Battery Reilly, buried on private property off Warren's Point Road adjacent to Briggs Marsh; and 3) South Reservation, Battery 212, at the end of Washington Road on Sakonnet Point. See chapter 6.

At the North or West Reservation (Battery Gray), the army installed two 16-inch guns (68 feet long and weighing 143 tons) on barbette carriages

On the left are the two batteries for 8-inch guns inside an artificial hill at Battery Reilly, circa 1942. *Dugan Family Collection, Fort Adams Trust.* On the right, a current view of the hill at former Battery Reilly. *Christopher Zeeman.*

within a bombproof and well-camouflaged casemate (550 feet long and 33,500 cubic feet). The casemates, located near the driving range of the Sakonnet Golf Club at 685 West Main Road, are covered with trees, shrubs and vines. All points of access have been sealed with earth. Only the ruins of the battery's fire-control tower remain visible.

The East Reservation (Battery Reilly) had two 8-inch seacoast guns emplaced in earth-covered concrete casemates (*41.475784, -71.171983*) similar in design and construction to Battery Gray but about one-third the size. The 74-acre reservation once contained nine barracks, mess halls, officers' headquarters, a store and a movie theater, as well as radar towers. Only the artificial hill that holds the concrete casemates is visible today; all openings are overgrown with grass turf.

The South Reservation (Battery 212) was located at Sakonnet Point. It consisted of two 6-inch barbette-mounted rapid-fire rifles. The ammunition magazine was situated between and slightly to the rear of the two guns in an earth-covered bombproof shelter 9,775 cubic feet in size. The guns had a range of fifteen miles. A private home was built on top of the artificial hill. One gun emplacement at one end of the hill has a swimming pool on top of it, and at the other end of the hill is a guesthouse. The concrete bunker is used by the owner for storage.

A fire-control station located on Warren Point, east of the Warren's Point Beach Club, is now a private residence at 15 Kempton Place (*41.461544, -71.170446*). This station likely held the SCR-296-A radar system assigned to Warren Point.

BLOCK ISLAND

Block Island Military Reservation, 576 Beach Avenue, New Shoreham, 41.178832, -71.569587

On an island some thirteen miles south of the mainland, Block Island residents were exposed to potential raids by German submarines and perhaps motor torpedo boats. They were advised to evacuate the island after the Pearl Harbor attack, but few did. See chapter 1, volume 1.

The Block Island Military Reservation, a two-acre camp located along Beach Avenue near Harbor Pond, was established. The army's Coast Artillery and Signal Corps used the site to watch for enemy planes and ships and to support the several fire-control, radar and searchlight stations on the island. The navy had a Harbor Detection Station on the island.

The facilities were manned by both the Narragansett Bay Harbor Defense Command and Eastern Long Island Sound Harbor Defense Command. There were no major gun batteries emplaced here. Four outlying sites around the island were used for fire-control stations for both harbor defense commands. A total of eight separate stations and cement lookout towers, along with two radar towers and a protected switchboard bunker, were built and disguised as silos and farmhouses. Spotters could provide coordinates for heavy artillery on the mainland to fire at enemy vessels.

Two tall fire-control towers were built fairly close to each other in the northern part of the island, at the Maze, the highest point of Corn Neck. They were blown up by the property owner in February 1976. Two other tall towers were built in the southern part of the island on Lewis Farm at Lewis Point at the end of Lewis Farm Road (near *41.149180, -71.596098*). One overlooked steep bluffs and was more than one-quarter of a mile to the southwest of the other one. They were demolished by the property owner in the early 1970s. Lewis Farm Road is an unmarked private dirt road just to the west of the Greenway.

The four surviving stations, consisting of cottages or silos, disguised to be "not conspicuous," are all now private residences:

- At 1054 Beacon Hill Road (*41.173482, -71.587663*). Beacon Hill Tower, built of stone on the highest point of the island in 1928 by the Doggett family, is visible from many places on the island. The property has stone columns marking its entrance. It was commandeered by the army for the war's duration shortly after the attack on Pearl Harbor. A switchboard used by soldiers during the war sits outside the old stone house. Next door stands a one-story summer cottage built by the army in the summer of 1944, with a two-story concrete fire-control post in its rear, with a northwest view.

- A one-story concrete fire-control structure with a northwest view was built onto a wooden cottage in the vicinity of 741 Corn Neck Road (*41.216443, -71.564937*).
- At 315 Spring Street (*41.158744, -71.548535*) is the only remaining cylindrical lookout tower on the island. It was a three-story "wood frame and reinforced concrete" structure used by mainland artillery for fire control. Vin McAloon recalled from his childhood that the tower had a conical top and was painted red to make it look like a silo. The tower is at the rear of a one-story concrete fire-control post with a southeast view.
- At 1629 Pilot Hill Road (*41.157391, -71.559631*), off of Payne Road, a two-story concrete extension to a wooden cottage served as a fire-control post, with a view of Montauk, Long Island.

Fire-control tower and building on Spring Street, on the southeast coast of Block Island. The cylindrical tower can be seen in the distance from the Southeast Lighthouse gift shop and south of the gift shop from Spring Street. *Christian McBurney*.

There was a radar tower near the Southeast Lighthouse designed to look like a water tank. A boulder now marks the former site of the lighthouse, which was built in 1873 and moved inland in 1993 (*41.15385, -71.55242*). A postwar photograph in the Southeast Lighthouse gift shop shows a concrete pad on the right near the end of the front yard; this pad may have been where the radar tower was located. A SCR 296-A radar system used for fire control for the heavy artillery on the mainland was located here in 1944. Soldiers manning this site would have seen the explosions from depth charges and hedgehogs fired by navy and coast guard ships on May 6, 1945, as they destroyed the last German U-boat sunk in the war. See chapter 13, volume 1. A SCR 296-A radar system was planned for the west side but never installed.

Because many of the existing World War II sites on Block Island stand on private property, the best way to view them is on a private tour arranged with the Block Island Historical Society.

Fall River, Massachusetts

Battleship Cove, 5 Water Street

Special mention is made of nearby Battleship Cove, a maritime museum and war memorial in Fall River that features the world's largest collection of World War II naval vessels. On board the battleship USS *Massachusetts*, visitors can view the huge 16-inch naval guns, similar to guns that were placed at Narragansett and Little Compton during the war. The battleship also carries Oerlikon-Gazda 20-millimeter antiaircraft guns (at the stern and near the bow) that were designed and manufactured in Rhode Island and employed on all types of navy vessels. See chapter 7, volume 1, and Pawtucket earlier. The *Lionfish* submarine displays torpedoes that may have been manufactured at the Naval Torpedo Station at Newport. See chapter 1, volume 1 and the Goat Island entry.

Only a few PT boats from World War II remain today. Two of them have been restored for display at the National PT Boat Museum at Battleship Cove. They also carry Oerlikon-Gazda 20-millimeter antiaircraft guns, as well as torpedoes that may have been manufactured at the Naval Torpedo Station at Newport.

Windsor Locks, Connecticut

New England Air Museum, 36 Perimeter Road

Special mention is also made of the New England Air Museum in Windsor Locks, north of Hartford. Among its World War II collections is an F6F-5 Hellcat, an aircraft commonly used by pilots training at Quonset Point, Charlestown and Westerly in 1944 and 1945. Other planes it has that were flown in Rhode Island during the war include a Grumman FM-2 Wildcat and the Vought XF4U-4 Corsair. It also has one of the U.S. Army's P-47 Thunderbolts. These planes flew out of Hillsgrove Army Air Base in Warwick. The museum has a Grumman TBM-3E Avenger awaiting restoration.

Rhode Island Winners of the Army-Navy "E" Award for Excellence in War Production

Company Name and Location	Number of Awards
Ashton (Cumberland)	
Owens-Corning Fiberglass Corp., Ashton Plant	4
Bristol	
United States Rubber Co., Bristol Plant	1
Central Falls	
Pantex Pressing Machine, Inc.	[not legible]
Cranston	
The Central Tool Co., Curtiss Engineering Co.	2
Respro, Inc.	2
Crompton (West Warwick)	
Boston Wire Stitcher, Crompton Plant	1
East Greenwich	
Boston Wire Stitcher, East Greenwich Plant	1

Company Name and Location	Number of Awards
East Providence	
Abrasive Machine Tool Co.	4
Mason Can Co.	3
Lonsdale (Lincoln)	
Lonsdale Co., Lincoln Bleachery and Dye Works Division	4
Newport	
U.S. Naval Torpedo Station	5
North Smithfield	
Uxbridge Worsted Co., Andrews Mill	4
Pascoag	
Uxbridge Worsted Co., Pascoag Mill	4
Pawtucket	
The A. O. G. Corp.	3
Fran Corp., Pawtucket Plant (includes Providence Plant)	2
Hemphill Co.	1
United Aircraft Corp., Hamilton Standard Propellers Division, Darlington Plant	[not legible]
Phillipsdale (East Providence)	
Kennecott Wire & Cable Co.	4
Providence	
B. A. Ballou & Co.	1
Brown & Sharpe Manufacturing Co., Providence Plant (also won Navy "E" Award prior to July 1942)	5
Builders Iron Foundry	4
Federal Products Corp.	4
Gorham Manufacturing Co.	2
Handy & Harmon, Providence Plant	5
Imperial Knife Co.	1
Adolph Mueller Co., Instrument Jewel Bearing Plant	1

COMPANY NAME AND LOCATION	NUMBER OF AWARDS
Providence (continued)	
Henry Owens & Co.	1
Rau Fastener Co.	3
Silverman Brothers	[not legible]
Standard Machinery Co.	2
Taco Heaters, Inc.	2
United States Rubber Co., Providence Plant	[not legible]
United Wire & Supply Corp.	4
Slatersville	
Kendall Co., Kendall Mills Division, Slatersville Plant	3
Warren	
The Anchorage, Inc.	1
Crown Fastener Corp.	3
Kleistone Rubber Co., Inc.	[not legible]
Westerly	
C.B. Cottrell & Sons Co.	3
George C. Moore Co.	4
Woonsocket	
Jacob Finkelstein & Sons	5
Taft-Peirce Manufacturing Co.	5
United States Rubber Co., Woonsocket Plant	1
Uxbridge Worsted Co., Glenark Mill	4

Source: David D. Jackson, "The American Automobile Industry in World War II," at http://usautoindustryworldwartwo.com/Army-Navy%20E%20Awards/Army-Navy%20E%20Awards-page-12.htm.

(Jacob Finkelstein & Sons and Taft Pierce Manufacturing Co. corrected, from 4 awards to 5)

APPENDIX B

A Sampling of Woonsocket Textile Mills and Their U.S. Army Contracts during World War II

(N.A. means information not available)

Company/ Division	Number of Employees	Known Information on Contracts Obtained (Dates of Contracts in Parentheses)
Airedale Worsted Mills	N.A.	(Suffered from strikes until 1945); 50,000 yards of 56-inch, 18-ounce piece dyed olive drab serge cloth (March 1945)
Bell Company of Worcester (Spinning Division)	490	$236,00 for uniform cloth (July 1941); $75,000 for uniform cloth (Oct. 1941); $531,900 for 270,00 yards of olive drab flannel shirting; $471,000 for serge cloth; $59,100 for 30,000 yards of 10.5 ounce shirting (Nov. 1941); $1,213,100 for 30,000 yards of 10.5-ounce shirting; 290,000 yards of 18-ounce wool serge; 50,000 yards of olive drab serge (Dec. 1941); 260,000 yards of worsted cloth (Dec. 1944)

Company/ Division	Number of Employees	Known Information on Contracts Obtained (Dates of Contracts in Parentheses)
Belmont Worsted	N.A.	$1,213,100 (all years)
Bonin Spinning	335	N.A.
Cherry Brook Worsted	235	N.A.
Dunn Worsted	400	$38,000 for 12,500 yards of serge cloth; $420,760 for serge cloth; $113,687 (Oct. 1941); $402,760 (Dec. 1941); 79,000 yards of 18-ounce serge cloth (Dec. 1944)
Guerin Mills	1,400 (Alsace Division 700 spinning yarn; Montrose Worsted Division 400 weaving; Rosemont Dyeing Division 150)	$840,000 of dark shade serge (April 1941); $876,000 for uniform cloth; 75,000 yards of 18-ounce light shade serge cloth; 25,000 yards of 18-ounce drab serge cloth (July 1941); $77,500 for 25,000 yards of olive drab serge cloth (Oct. 1941); $1,256,000) (Dec. 1941)
Jacob Finkelstein & Sons (Samoset Mill)	500	N.A.
Lippitt Woolen Company	N.A.	$184,937 (Oct. 1941); $217,360 (Nov. 1941); $327,260 (Dec. 1941)
Onawa Mill	410	N.A.
Sadwin Manufacturing	Added 35	Abdominal belts (Nov. 1941)
Sidney Blumenthal Manufacturing	450	N.A.

Company/ Division	Number of Employees	Known Information on Contracts Obtained (Dates of Contracts in Parentheses)
Verdun Manufacturing Company	N.A.	$105,300 of dark shade serge (April 1941); $61,250 for 25,000 yards, 18-ounce olive drab serge; $114,750; $157,000 (years N.A.)
Winsor Manufacturing		$17,050 for 967,000 olive drab handkerchiefs; $23,900 white cotton handkerchiefs (years N.A.); 467,000 drab handkerchiefs (Dec. 1944)
Worcester Textile Co. (Greystone Mill)	N.A.	$286,500 of dark shade serge (April 1941)

Woonsocket companies known to have received military contracts, but about which no other specific contract information is known: American Woolen Company (Saranac Mill); Barnai Worsted Co.; Cumberland Worsted; French Worsted Company; Lafayette Worsted Company; Riverside Worsted Company; Uxbridge Worsted Company (Glenark Mill).

Sources: *Providence Journal*, June 21, 1940; July 26, 1940; October 5, 1940; April 6, 1941; June 1, 1941; November 30, 1941; September 1, 1944; September 27, 1944; December 17, 1944; March 1, 1945; March 16, 1945; March 18, 1945.

Bibliography

Chapter 1: President Franklin D. Roosevelt Inspects Newport, August 1940

Periodicals

Morgan, Thomas. "President Roosevelt Visits Newport to Check Out the Fleet. His Thoughts Turn to Seapower as War Clouds Scud Nearer." *Providence Journal*, August 12, 1990.

Original Sources

Brooklyn Eagle. "F.D.R. Inspects Torpedo Plant in Tour Windup." August 12, 1940.

Newport Daily News. "Apprentice Total to Be Increased." August 16, 1940.

———. "Newport Naval Spread Considered." August 16, 1940.

Newport Mercury. "Constellation Again in Full Commission." August 30, 1940.

Providence Journal. "Roosevelt, Knox Impressed by Inspection at Newport." August 13, 1940.

Salt Lake Tribune (Salt Lake City, UT). "Roosevelt Completes Tour of Northeastern Defenses." August 13, 1940 (Associated Press report).

Chapter 2: Admirals King and Ingersoll Command the Atlantic Fleet from Newport

Books

Buell, Thomas B. *Master of Seapower. A Biography of Fleet Admiral Ernest J. King.* Annapolis, MD: Naval Institute Press, 1980.

Love, Robert William, Jr. *The Chiefs of Naval Operations.* Annapolis, MD: Naval Institute Press, 1980.

Symonds, Craig L. *World Word II at Sea: A Global History*. New York: Oxford University Press, 2018.

Toll, Ian W. *Pacific Crucible: War at Sea in the Pacific, 1941–1942.* New York: W.W. Norton & Company, 2012.

Periodicals

Obituary (Royal E. Ingersoll). *New York Times*, May 22, 1976.

Sanders, Vice Admiral H. "King of the Oceans." *United States Naval Institute Proceedings Magazine* 100 (August 1974): 52–59. (Sanders served as an aide to King in Newport).

Original Sources

Baltimore Sun. "Ingersoll of the Atlantic Fleet." February 28, 1943.

Franklin D. Roosevelt White House Calendar, December 10 and 16, 1941. www.fdrlibrary.marist.edu/daybyday/daylog.

Newport Mercury. "Rotary Club Hears Commander Davis." August 14, 1942.

Other Sources

Kohnen, David (Executive Director of the Naval War College Museum). Email to Christian McBurney, December 2, 2017, regarding Admiral King on December 7, 1941.

"Ingersoll, Royal E." and "King, Ernest J." Naval History and Heritage Command, www.history.navy.mil.

Wikipedia. "USS *Vixen* (PG-53)." https://en.wikipedia.org/wiki/USS_Vixen_(PG-53).

C<small>HAPTER</small> 3: C<small>HOPMIST</small> H<small>ILL</small> L<small>ISTENING</small> P<small>OST</small>: R<small>HODE</small> I<small>SLAND'S</small> S<small>PY</small> S<small>TATION</small>

Books

Eno, Paul F., and Glenn V. Laxton. *Rhode Island, a Genial History*. Woonsocket, RI: New River Press, 2005.

Periodicals

Caisse, Leo. "Ears on the World." *America in WWII* (October 2017): 23–27.

Kneitel, Tom. "CB's Secret Wartime Mission, The Day They Heard Nazi Panzers on 11-Meters!" *CB Radio* (February 1978): 20–24.

Providence Journal, various articles. November 23, 1945; December 6, 1981; April 21, 1983; January 24, 1946; January 26, 1946; February 11, 1946; February 21, 1951; April 21, 1983; August 9, 2015.

Other Sources

Rydberg, Allen. "Chopmist Listening Post." The Online Review of Rhode Island History, www.smallstatebighistory.com.

Sterling, George E. "The History of the Radio Intelligence Division Before and During World War II." Articles gathered by Albert A. Evangelista, E. Merle Glunt, and Dan Flanagan. Updated 2012. Available online at http://users.isp.com/danflan/sterling/ridhist.pdf. (Sterling was the chief of the Radio Intelligence Division of the FCC during World War II.)

Wikipedia. "Chopmist Hill Listening Post." https://en.wikipedia.org/wiki/Chopmist_Hill_Listening_Post.

CHAPTER 4: JOHN F. KENNEDY TRAINS AT MELVILLE, OCTOBER 1942 TO JANUARY 1943

Books

Breur, William B. *Sea Wolf, A Biography of John D. Bulkeley, USN.* Novato, CA: Presidio Press, 1989.

Donovan, Robert J. *PT 109: John F. Kennedy in World War II.* New York: McGraw Hill, 1961.

Doyle, William. *PT 109, An American Epic of War, Survival, and the Destiny of John F. Kennedy.* New York: William Morrow, 2005.

Original Sources

Frost, Donald B. Interview by Vicki Daitch, January 26, 2005. John F. Kennedy Library.

Liebenow, William F. "Bud." Interview by Vicki Daitch, February 15, 2005. John F. Kennedy Library.

CHAPTER 5: WOONSOCKET'S MILLS PRODUCE UNIFORMS, FAKE RUBBER TANKS AND MORE FOR THE WAR EFFORT

Books

Bacon, Raymond H. *Toward the New Millennium: Woonsocket, Rhode Island.* Woonsocket, RI: Woonsocket Centennial Committee, 2000.

Fortin, Marcel P., and Woonsocket Centennial Committee. *Woonsocket, Rhode Island: A Centennial History, 1888–2000, the Millennium Edition.* Woonsocket, RI: Woonsocket Centennial Committee, 2000.

Kulik, Gary, et al. *Rhode Island: An Inventory of Historic Engineering and Industrial Sites.* U.S. Department of the Interior, Heritage Conservation and Recreation Service, Office of Archeology and Historic Preservation. Historic American Engineering Record, 1978.

Rhode Island Historical Preservation Commission. Woonsocket, Rhode Island. Providence: Rhode Island Historical Preservation Commission, 1976.

Periodicals

Hill, John. "The Art of War: Woonsocket Mill Supplied Allied Forces of Deception Against Nazis." *Providence Journal,* June 5, 2017.

Smith, Michael. "Secret 'Weapons' Crafted at a Rhode Island Mill Instrumental to D-Day Success." *Brownsville Herald,* June 6, 2001 (Knight Ridder Report).

Original Sources

Courier (Waterloo, IA). "Landing Craft for Which Parts Were Made in Waterloo Put United States Soldiers onto Invasion Beaches Around the World." September 30, 1943 (Associated Press report).

Finkelstein, Rick. Interview by Norman Desmarais, July 18, 2018.

Portsmouth (NH) Herald. "Name R.I. Man President of N.E. Council." November 16, 1944.

Other Sources

National Register of Historic Places registration applications for various mills and historic districts.

CHAPTER 6: MORE STORIES FROM WESTERLY, CHARLESTOWN, JAMESTOWN, NEWPORT, LITTLE COMPTON, PROVIDENCE AND PAWTUCKET

Books

Conn, Stetson, Rose C. Engleman and Byron Fairchild. *Guarding the United States and Its Outposts*. Washington, D.C.: Center of Military History, United States Army, 2000.

Lisle, Janet. *The History of Little Compton, A Home by the Sea, 1820–1950*. Little Compton, RI: Little Compton Historical Society, 2012.

Periodicals

Baker, Frank. "Sun Sets on Unique Sunday Newspaper. Journalism: Rhode Island Paper Converts to Morning Publication Today." Associated Press announcement, April 2, 1995.

Fusaro, Nancy Burns. "Sun's Historic Scoop Included Rewrite of History in Making." *Westerly Sun*, December 7, 2016.

Original Sources

Baltimore Sun. "Walsh Called Isolationist." October 31, 1944.

Chicago Tribune. "Honor Ensign for Rescuing Sailor at Sea." August 26, 1945.

Newport Mercury. "Signalman Cited for Aiding Fliers." March 31, 1944.

North Kingstown Death Records, North Kingstown Town Clerk's Office (James Gilmore Canning).

Providence Sunday Journal. "First Pictures of Big Guns of Narragansett Bay Harbor Defenses." April 21, 1946.

Quonset Scout. "Award Sought for Pilot Who Saved Crewman." May 11, 1945.

————. "Bravery of Charlestown Sailor Is Rewarded." June 7, 1944.

Tampa Bay Tribune. "Truman Calls for Election of Roosevelt." October 31, 1944, 2 (Associated Press report).

Westerly Sun. "Rewarded for Heroic Deed." January 16, 1944.

————. "Saw Plane Crash, Shore Road Men Rush to Scene." October 25, 1943.

Ziemer, Howard Ziemer. "My Navy Career." Unpublished memoir. World War II Veterans Project, at www.memory.loc.gov.

Other Sources

Fort Burnside display at the Beavertail Lighthouse Museum, Jamestown, Rhode Island (C.A. Wood).

Ignasher, Jim. "Westerly, Rhode Island—October 24, 1943." New England Aviation History, www.newenglandaviationhistory.com.

CHAPTER 7: GEORGE H.W. BUSH TRAINS AT CHARLESTOWN, NOVEMBER 1943 TO JANUARY 1944

Books

Hyams, Joe. *Flight of the Avenger. George Bush at War.* San Diego, CA: Harcourt Brace Jovanovich, 1991.

Stinnett, Robert B. *George Bush: His World War II Years.* Washington, D.C.: Brassey's (US) Inc., 1992.

Original Sources

George Bush Correspondence, November 30, 1943–January 23, 1944, George H.W. Bush Presidential Library.

Meakin, Harold D. Letter to the editor, January 14, 1994, in *Westerly Sun*, January 25, 1994.

Other Sources

"Bush, George H.W." Naval History and Heritage Command, www.history.navy.mil.

CHAPTER 8: CHILDHOOD MEMORIES OF THE HOMEFRONT AT QUONOCHONTAUG

Books

Conn, Stetson, Rose C. Engleman and Byron Fairchild. *Guarding the United States and Its Outposts*. Washington, D.C.: Center of Military History, United States Army, 2000.

Doyle, Anne Schafer. *Quonnie: People, Places and Pathways. A Self-Guided Historic Walking /Driving Tour of Quonochontaug, Rhode Island*. Privately printed, 4th ed., 2011.

Original Sources

Balcezak, Ted. Interview by Christian McBurney, June 28, 2018.

Battista, Tom. Email to Christian McBurney, June 28, 2018.

Bettinger, Fredericka. Interview by Christian McBurney, September 5, 2019.

Houle, Charlotte. Video presentation at the Quonochontaug Historical Society, summer 2017. Video taken by Robert Petrone.

Jones, Crispin. *Quonnie: Legends & History*. Quonochontaug, RI: Privately printed, 2018.

Mageau, James M. "Life in Cross's Mills During World War Two." April 2016. Copy at the Charlestown Historical Society.

Moore, Dave. "Memories of a Boy Growing Up at Watch Hill During World War II." The Online Review of Rhode Island History, www.smallstatebighistory.com.

Sayer, Edmund. Emails to R. Peter Mogielnicki, May 1 and July 17, 2018.

Unidentified elderly man at a lecture at Kingston Free Library, June 18, 2017. Interview by Christian McBurney about the firing of the 16-inch gun at Narragansett.

Wholean, Bill, Carol Waterman and Dick Hutchins. Interviews by Anne Doyle, 2002. Quonochontaug Historical Society.

CHAPTER 9: SEABEES TEST A PONTOON AIRFIELD ON NARRAGANSETT BAY

Books

Building the Navy's Bases in World War II. History of the Bureau of Yards and Docks and the Civil Engineer Corps, 1940–1946. Vol. 1. Washington, D.C.: Government Printing Office, 1947. (Pontoons discussed at pages 156–60.)

Original Sources

Pontoon Gear Manual. Washington, D.C.: Government Printing Office, 1944.

"U.S. Navy Project SOCK (December 1942–February 1944)." Undated summary (prepared by the Department of Defense, circa 1963), archives, U.S. Navy Seabee Museum.

Other Sources

"Captain John N. Laycock." Naval History and Heritage Command, U.S. Navy Seabee Museum, www.history.navy.mil.

Rogers, J. David (professor at Missouri University of Science & Technology, Rolla, Missouri). Email correspondence with Christian McBurney, April 22–May 5, 2019.

————. "Navy Seabee Operations Pacific Theater During World War II." Missouri University of Science and Technology, https://web.mst.edu.

CHAPTER 10: A CONNECTICUT WAVE AT QUONSET POINT

Original Sources

The narrative was recorded by Marie Duggins's daughter, Linda McAuliffe, who interviewed her mother at various times from May 29 to June 7, 2016. Linda transcribed the draft and double-checked it with Marie. Christian McBurney edited the narrative. Marie Duggins passed away on March 9, 2017, at the age of ninety-seven.

CHAPTER 11: MORE STORIES FROM QUONSET POINT AND DAVISVILLE

Books

Ambrose, Stephen E. *Nixon. The Education of a Politician, 1913–1962.* New York: Simon and Schuster, 1987.

100 Fighting Ships Built During World War II by Herreshoff, Bristol, Rhode Island. Privately printed, 1945.

Original Sources

Asselin, Hector. Interview by Linsey Lee, February 11, 2002. Oral history collection, Martha's Vineyard Museum.

Helwig, Marion Cheever. Interview by Christian McBurney, June 18, 2017.

J. Allen Bell to his wife, July 26, 1944. Collection of Christian McBurney.

Newport Mercury. "British Flier Killed Near Here Identified." July 30, 1943.

Public Papers of the Presidents of the United States, Richard Nixon, 1973. Washington, D.C.: Government Printing Office, 1975. Remarks on presenting the Presidential Medal of Freedom to William P. Rogers, October 15, 1973.

Quonset Scout. "Grateful Pilots Tip Packers." April 19, 1944.

———. "Packer Is a Grandma" July 23, 1943.

Other Sources

"Nixon, Richard M." Naval History and Heritage Command, www.history. navy.mil.

Chapter 12: Harbor Entrance Command Post at Fort Burnside in Jamestown

Books

Berhow, Mark, ed. "Guide to Controlled Mines." In *American Seacoast Defenses, A Reference Guide.* Bel Air, MD: CDSG Press, 1999.

Conn, Stetson, Rose C. Engleman and Byron Fairchild. *Guarding the United States and Its Outposts.* Washington, D.C.: Center of Military History, United States Army, 2000.

Schroder, Walter K. *The Defenses of Narragansett Bay.* Rhode Island Publications Society, 1980.

Periodicals

Coastal Defense Study Group Journal Excerpts. Various dates. Walter Schroder Collection (accessed in 2000).

Original Sources

Beezer, Mark, Edward Morino, Walter Schroder and John Quattromani. Interview of these Jamestown residents about Fort Burnside by Varoujan Karentz. Various dates in 2000 and 2001. Jamestown Historical Society.

COE Mine Renovations. Record Group 77. National Archives Center, Waltham, Massachusetts.

Gatchell, Colonel Theodore. Transcript of discussions on the Rhode Island National Guard. April 2001. Naval War College, Newport, Rhode Island.

MacDougald, Joseph (former HECP duty officer at Fort Burnside). Interview by Varoujan Karentz, April 27 and May 30, 2000. Karentz Papers, Jamestown Historical Society.

———. Letters of Memorandum. National Archives, Wrentham, Massachusetts.

McNally, Irwin (former Commander). Letters of Memorandum to Norm Kim, Aug. 7, 1995. Raytheon Company Archives, Wayland MA.

Smith, Bowling. Interview by Coastal Defense Study Group at McLean, VA. April 10, 2001. Emailed to author.

Stern, Colonel I. Henry (former commanding officer of Fort Burnside). Interview by Varoujan Karentz, August 20 and 26, 1998.

Stevens, Joseph (of the World War II Museum in Kodiak, Alaska). Email correspondence with Varoujan Karentz on U.S. coastal defense, various dates, 2000.

Zink, Robert D. Email correspondence with Varoujan Karentz on controlled submarine mines used in the United States, various dates in 2001.

Other Sources

Fort Wiki. "Northeastern WWII Radar Sites." www.fortwiki.com.

History of Harbor Entrance Control Posts. Undated. Commandant First Naval District. Boston, Massachusetts

243rd Coast Artillery Pictorial Review. Providence, Rhode Island State Archives.

Chapter 13: Beavertail's Top Secret Spraycliff Observatory and Charlestown's Brash Night Fighters

Books

Coletta, Paolo. *United States Navy and Marine Corps Bases*. Westport, CT: Greenwood Press, 1985.

Grumman Aircraft Co. *History of Grumman Aircraft's Naval Fighter of WW II, F6F Hellcat*. Long Island, NY: Calverton, 1992.

"Radar." In *International Military and Defense Encyclopedia*, ed. Col. Trevor N. Dupuy. Vol. 5. Washington, D.C.: Brassey's (US), 1993, 2237–38.

Ridenour, L.N., ed. *Radiation Laboratory Series*. Vol. 1. New York: McGraw-Hill, 1947–53.

Schroder, Walter K. *Defenses of Narragansett Bay in World War II*. Rhode Island Publications Society, 1980.

Tillman, Barrett. *Hellcat: The F6F in World War II*. Annapolis, MD: Naval Institute Press, 1979.

―――. *King of the Pacific Fighters*. Pacific Fighters, Air Combat Stories. Air Age Publishing, 2003.

Woodbury, David O. *Battlefronts of Industry*. *Westinghouse in World War II*. Hoboken, NJ: John Wiley & Sons, 1948.

Periodicals

"The MIT Radiation Laboratory: RLE's Microwave Heritage." *RLE Currents* 4, no. 2 (Spring 1992).

Parish, Karl. "Mickey and the Night Fighters." *Naval History* 17, no. 6 (December 2003).

Original Sources

Cotel-Templeton, Anna. Interview by Varoujan Karentz, August 2011, on Beavertail land transfers.

Dungan, Fred, Paul Kepple, John Gilman and Archie Stockebrand. Interview of these members of Squadron VN (N) 76 who trained at Charlestown Naval Auxiliary Facility, August 2003. Transcript and audio recording at Jamestown Historical Society.

Land Evidence Records, Beavertail Deeds. Town Clerk's Office, Town Hall, Jamestown, Rhode Island.

N51-209 File. U.S Navy Nacelle Radars. MIT Museum, Cambridge, Massachusetts.

Newport Daily News. "Beavertail Unit Expansion." May 18, 1950.

Osborne, James. Interview by Varoujan Karentz, June–July 2011, on radar communications.

Photograph caption, File Number 48783, April 8, 1945, U.S. Navy. National Archives, Washington, D.C.

Spraycliff. Logs and Progress Reports. 1943. National Archives, Waltham, Massachusetts.

U.S. Army Corps of Engineers. Communications Site Investigation Report, April 22, 1994.

U.S. Army Corps of Engineers. Site Survey Report Fort Burnside, June 24, 1994.

Zecchino, Paul. Interview by Varoujan Karentz on radar and communications, June 2011.

CHAPTER 14: EDWARD SWAIN HOPE, THE NAVY'S FIRST BLACK LIEUTENANT, TRAINS AT DAVISVILLE

Books

MacGregor, Morris J. *Integration of the Armed Forces, 1940–1965.* Defense Studies Series. Washington, D.C.: Center of Military History, United States Army, 1981.

Original Sources

Loveridge, G.Y. "Navy's First Negro Lieutenant Now on Duty in Rhode Island." *Providence Sunday Journal*, October 8, 1944.

New York Age. "Negro Engineer Sworn in Lieutenant in U.S. Navy." May 20, 1944.

Of sports, only boxing was integrated: *See, e.g., Quonset Scout,* June 14, 1945; July 19, 1945.

Segregated dances for black navy sailors: *See, e.g., Quonset Scout,* July 5, 1945; August 9 and 16, 1945.

Sherber, Evelyn. "Lt. Edward Swain Hope Shatters Navy Tradition." *Pittsburgh Courier,* July 8, 1944.

Stiles, Joseph. Interview by Linsey Lee, June 28, 2002. Oral history collection, Martha's Vineyard Museum.

Summary Report on Facilities, Naval Aviation Shore Establishments, Bureau of Aeronautics, Air Station Branch—Shore Establishment Group—Maintenance Division, Government Printing Office, 1945.

Other Sources

"LCDR Edward Swain Hope." Naval Heritage and History Command, U.S. Navy Seabee Museum, www.history.navy.mil.

Chapter 15: Could *U-853*'s Sinking of *Black Point* Have Been Averted?

Original Sources

Bradley, John G. Interview by Christian McBurney, July 2, 2018.

———. Interview by Scott R. Stets of Phoenix Rising Films, 2010. YouTube. www.youtube.com.

Hartford Courant. "Angus and [John G.] Bradley Awarded Commissions." November 9, 1944.

War Diary of Torpedo Squadron 44, from April 5, 1945 to June 30, 1945 (Brinson). www.fold3.com.

Chapter 16: Elisabeth Sheldon: Her Summers of 1944 and 1945 on Narragansett Bay

Original Sources

Aschman, Elisabeth "Betty" Sheldon. Interview by Christian McBurney, May 28, 2016. After residing in Saunderstown, Elisabeth passed away on August 8, 2019, at the age of ninety-five.

———. Scrapbook. Includes (i) Elisabeth K. Sheldon Sailing Permit, June 6, 1944; (ii) news clippings of two stories, in unidentified newspapers, probably dated some time in 1945, one announcing the death of Jim Bistodeau and the other the death of Otho Edwards, and (iii) letter from Forbes Whiteside to Betty Sheldon, October 3, 1945.

MacDonald, Louise Sheldon. Email to Christian McBurney, April 18, 2016, and interview by him, August 8, 2016.

Other Sources

MacDonald, Louise Sheldon. "Encounters with Myself." (draft of autobiography), circa 2016.

CHAPTER 17: WAR HERO DIXIE KIEFER'S FINAL BOW AT QUONSET POINT

Periodicals

Levine, David. "The Indestructible Man: The Story of Dixie Kiefer." *Hudson Valley Magazine*, November 1, 2015.

Original Sources

Quonset Scout. "Station Pays Last Tribute to Commodore Kiefer, Air Crash Victim." November 15, 1945.

———. "Waves, Sailors, Thrilled at News, Pray in Chapel." August 23, 1945.

Other Sources

"Dixie Kiefer, Commodore, United States Navy." Arlington National Cemetery, www.arlingtoncemetery.net/dixie-kiefer.htm.

"Kiefer, Dixie." Naval History and Heritage Command, www.history.navy.mil.

Index

About the Authors

Each of the authors is also a contributing author to the Online Review of Rhode Island History at www.smallstatebighistory.com. To find articles by them, go to the website, click on the Archives tab and review the list of articles, or type in the author's name in the search box.

CHRISTIAN MCBURNEY, the primary editor of this book and the editor and publisher of the Online Review of Rhode Island History, has written seven books on Rhode Island and/or Revolutionary War history, including *The Rhode Island Campaign: The First French and American Operation of the Revolutionary War* and *Spies in Revolutionary Rhode Island*. For more information on his books and lectures go to www.christianmcburney.com.

NORMAN DESMARAIS is the author of Guide to the American Revolutionary War series (six volumes about the war on land and seven volumes about the war at sea and overseas). He is also the author of the recent book *America's First Ally: France in the American Revolutionary War* and translator of the journal of Louis François Bertrand Dupont d'Aubevoye de Lauberdière, who was General Rochambeau's nephew and aide-de-camp. During World War II, Norm's father served as a chief petty officer aboard the heavy cruiser USS *Tuscaloosa*, which was sometimes stationed in Narragansett Bay.

ABOUT THE AUTHORS

VAROUJAN KARENTZ, since his retirement as a military radar/missile systems engineer and corporate officer of a major electronics manufacturer, has written several books, including *Beavertail Light Station on Conanicut Island*; *The Life Savers, Rhode Island's Forgotten Service*; and *Mitchnapert the Citadel, A History of Armenians in Rhode Island*. He was a board member of Heritage Harbor Museum, Beavertail Lighthouse Museum, member of Jamestown Historical Society and the recipient of the Rhode Island Antoinette F. Downing Volunteer Award for historic preservation accomplishments.